Praise for Diane Rehm's

On My Own

"Will invite comparisons to Joan Didion's own memoir of loss, *The Year of Magical Thinking*."
—*The Guardian*

"[A] clearheaded yet emotional call for national right-
to-die laws." —*Washington City Paper*

"Rehm writes eloquently about the changing landscape of grief, not only her own sorrow but that of
friends." —*The Kansas City Star*

"Brave and uplifting." —*Kirkus Reviews*

"Walks readers through the most recent year of
[Rehm's] life, struggling with living alone and figur-
ing out a new identity."
—*The Philadelphia Inquirer*

Diane Rehm

On My Own

Diane Rehm hosted *The Diane Rehm Show* on WAMU 88.5 FM in Washington, D.C.—distributed by NPR—from 1979 to 2016, when it had a weekly listening audience of two and a half million. She lives in Washington, D.C.

www.thedianerehmshow.org

On My Own

Our twenty-fifth wedding anniversary, 1984

DIANE REHM

On My Own

VINTAGE BOOKS

A Division of Penguin Random House LLC

New York

FIRST VINTAGE BOOKS EDITION, FEBRUARY 2017

The Library of Congress has catalogued the Knopf edition as follows:
Rehm, Diane.
On my own / Diane Rehm.—First edition.
pages cm
1. Rehm, Diane.   2. Radio broadcasters—United States—Biography.
3. Widows—United States—Biography.   4. Bereavement—United States.   5. Loss (Psychology)   6. Adjustment (Psychology)   7. Rehm, John B.—Health.   8. Parkinson's disease—Patients—Family relationships.
I. Title.
PN1991.4.R438A3 2015   791.4402'892—dc23   [B]   2015023006

Vintage Books Trade Paperback ISBN: 978-1-101-97364-6
eBook ISBN: 978-1-101-87529-2

Book design by Iris Weinstein

www.vintagebooks.com

Printed in the United States of America
10 9 8 7 6 5 4 3 2 1

This book is dedicated to the memory of John Rehm

On My Own

∼ A Decision

On June 14, 2014, my husband, John Rehm—age eighty-three—began his withdrawal from life. The aides at Brighton Gardens were instructed to stop bringing medications, menus, or water. His decision to die came after a long and difficult conversation the day before with Dr. Roy Fried, his primary physician; our son, David; our daughter, Jennifer, who was on the phone from Boston; and me.

John declared to Dr. Fried that because Parkinson's disease had so affected him that he no longer had the use of his hands, arms, or legs, because he could no longer stand, walk, eat, bathe, or in any way care for himself on his own, he was now ready to die. He said that he understood the disease was progressing, taking him further and further into incapacity, with no hope of improvement. Therefore, he wanted to end his life.

Clearly, his expectation—and his misunderstanding—was that, now that he had made his decision, he could simply be "put to sleep" immediately, with medication. When Dr. Fried explained that he was unable to carry out John's wishes, that he was prohibited from committing such an act in the state of Maryland, John became very angry. He said, "I feel *betrayed*." Tears came into his eyes, tears of frustration and disappointment. Here was a man who had lived his life able, for the most part, to take charge of events, to be certain that his well-considered decisions would be carried out. And now he was making the *ultimate* decision, and having it thwarted.

It was then that Dr. Fried explained that the only alternative John had, if he truly wished to die, was to stop eating, drinking fluids, or taking medications. In other words, he could bring his life to an end through those means, but no one could do it *for* him. Dr. Fried added that he hoped John would *not* make the decision to end his life, but that, if he did so, as his physician he would honor it.

My husband had moved into assisted living at Brighton Gardens in Chevy Chase, Maryland, in November 2012, because he could no longer stand or walk without falling, or care for himself without assistance. We'd spent months talking about the decision we both knew was coming. We went over and over various possibilities, such as having someone move into our apartment to care for him on a twenty-four-hour basis, but we knew that wouldn't work: there was simply not enough room for another human to be here full-time.

Most days I spent part of the afternoon with John at Brighton Gardens. Sometimes we'd sit silently, particularly in the weeks immediately after he moved in. Although he never admitted feeling resentful, it was clear he was unhappy. He had a private room, but was now in an institution, in the company of strangers, eating foods he didn't care for in a large communal dining room, and feeling an extreme loss of privacy. But slowly he regained his sense of humor, his interest in world events, and his happiness each time I walked through the door.

Over the years, John and I had talked many times about how we wanted to die. We had promised that we would do everything we could to support each other's wishes in the face of debilitating and unalterable conditions. Yet here I was, helpless to keep my promise. I could do nothing but listen as he railed against a medical and judicial system that prohibited a doctor from helping him die, even knowing that what awaited him was prolonged misery, further decline, and, to his mind, loss of dignity.

So John did what I dreaded, but knew in my heart he would do: he declared he would stop eating, drinking, or taking medications. He asked Dr. Fried how long the process of dying would last and was told it could be ten days to two weeks. John wanted to know, "Will I be in pain?" "Absolutely not," responded Dr. Fried. "I promise you, you will be kept comfortable."

A few months before this, John had come down with what's so often been called the old man's blessing. I was in South America, on a cruise with NPR listeners. It was a Saturday evening in March, and before I went to join the group for dinner, I called Brighton Gardens to check in. Our dear friends David and Mary Beth Busby were there with John, and Mary Beth answered the phone. When I asked how John was, she said, to my shock, "He's not responsive." I wasn't sure I was hearing correctly. "What do you mean, Mary Beth?" "Well, just that," she said. The two of them had been sitting there with John for an hour or so, and he was simply not moving; he was in a deep sleep, not responding to their questions, not moving when they prodded him. I asked her to feel his head. "Warm," she said. I immediately called Dr. Fried, who instructed an aide to take his temperature. It was 101.5 degrees. Dr. Fried said John was probably experiencing pneumonia. Urgently I demanded to know what he would do next. Dr. Fried said he would order oral antibiotics for him, but warned it could be four hours before they arrived, and that John might not be able to swallow them. At this point, I lost all composure. I screamed into the phone, "But he could be *dead* in four hours!" Dr. Fried then said he would go to a nearby pharmacy to obtain an injectable form of antibiotic, which he did, taking it to Brighton Gardens that night and giving John what may have been a lifesaving dose of the drug. It was 6:30 Saturday evening, and I was in Buenos Aires. I tried to get a flight out that very evening, but it was too late, so I flew to Miami the next night and then home to Washington on Monday.

By the time I arrived, John had responded well to the medication and was making a good recovery. All of our friends, as well as our son, David, who had hovered over him during the critical period of my absence, were amazed and delighted at the turnaround.

Sadly, within three weeks of my return, pneumonia again crept into John's lungs. Whether it was a remnant of the first infection or a brand-new one, he was again feverish, coughing, and exhibiting all the other symptoms he'd had earlier. He was put back on antibiotics, this time for a longer period.

After the second bout of pneumonia, and lengthy and extraordinarily frank and compassionate discussions with Dr. Fried and me, John said he no longer wished to be treated with antibiotics should he experience pneumonia yet again. He was clearly in a more weakened state.

Two months later, he was placed under hospice care, which meant the doctor had concluded that he had six months or less to live. John had already made clear his wishes for "comfort care only."

And so on June 14, John began to carry out his decision to withdraw from life. Some of the aides at Brighton Gardens were clearly uncomfortable with the instructions to cease bringing all food, water, and medications, and during the first two days came to see him, asking whether he didn't want to change his mind. John said "No" pleasantly, even cheerfully, as though, somehow, he had taken back his life and could do with it as he chose. So I sat by my husband's side as he slowly died.

I rage at a system that would not allow John to be helped toward his own death. He was of rational mind, with no hope of recovery, knowing full well that the only way ahead was a slow downward slide, moving toward more incapacity and even greater indignity. Why should it be that only a few states allow aid in dying with help from a trained physician willing to offer the ultimate gift? Why should my husband have to starve himself to death? I wonder, too, why John should have had to be so alone in the dying process. I cry at the loss of what might have been this final intimacy between us, replaced by a long descent into oblivion, unaware of his family and friends beside him offering him a loving farewell and wishing him a peaceful journey.

On the day John made his decision, I brought him a photograph album I'd made for him many years earlier recording his childhood and youth, from his birth in Paris, where his mother and dad had met, to his graduation from Friends Seminary in New York. He loved seeing the photos of the pond near the little house in France where he had spent the first six years of his life. His father worked the night shift at the *Paris Herald Tribune,* and therefore slept a good part of every day. John remembered attending a small French school at age three, and having the teacher put a pen into his hand on the very first day.

That hour, as I sat beside him on his bed going through the photographs, was extraordinary. Here was a man who had just decided he wanted to end his life experiencing so much joy as he reflected on his early years, while I, as I always had, adored gazing at his baby pictures. He was a beautiful child and a beautiful young man.

We had spent many months reflecting on our marriage, our life together, the joys and sadness we had shared, recalling many special moments of closeness, particularly sexually. But I wondered why we had wasted so much time in conflict with each other.

Out of those conversations came some starkly frank admissions from John, including a tearful confession of what he called his "deliberately emotionally abusive behavior" toward me. I was stunned at his bold words, having always wondered whether this behavior came from some deep desire to wound me—or to wound someone else. My suspicion had been that I was the mother against whom he had never rebelled.

That this admission came from John at nearly the end of his life almost made me leave the room in tears. How much anger, how much hostility had been directed at me, in the form of silence and withdrawal, how much frustration I had experienced with his denial of love and kindness on so many occasions, and now, on his deathbed, he was acknowledging to me that his behavior had been deliberate, and intended to wound me. I can still recall the pain I felt after he uttered those words, the desire to run from the room and give myself time to breathe. But here was the man I loved, leaving me with what I suspect he felt was a final "gift" of confession, one that he believed would take away the questions I'd long had in my mind as to why we had had such a difficult marriage.

What could I say? I told him I forgave him, and said I knew that I, too, had not always behaved in constructive ways. I asked him why he thought he had acted as he did, constantly withdrawing into silence, refusing to engage with me for weeks at a time. He simply said, "I don't know." I asked whether he thought he should have married at all. "Perhaps not," he said. "I always knew I was a loner. But then I would have missed out on so much in my life—you, David, and Jennie." He said he thought he might have spent his life reading, listening to music, writing poetry, disengaged from the people and the world around him, much as he had lived his early years in France.

I will always remember those conversations. Had John died suddenly, I would never have heard such words of regret from him, never heard him acknowledge how much our marriage and family had meant to him, or how our life together had changed him as a human being. They were so incredibly important to me and clearly to him as well.

From Saturday, June 14, through late Monday afternoon the sixteenth, John said he felt fine, "quite well, in fact." But by Monday evening, he was beginning what he had envisioned as "the long glide." He fell into a deep sleep and only occasionally made gestures with his face or his arms. His lips became parched. Either I or Musa Bangura, his faithful caregiver, would apply lotion. When we offered him chips of ice, he refused them, signaling that he didn't appreciate the cold. But there were tiny square sponges we could put into his mouth, to moisten his inner jaws and lips. Those seemed to comfort him.

On Wednesday, June 18, Jennie, an internist at the Lahey Clinic in Boston, flew in, and David drove down from Emmitsburg, Maryland, where he is provost at Mount St. Mary's University. Jennie walked into the room, put her hand in her father's, and said she felt sure he responded when she squeezed his hand. That was the last time Jennie was able to see her dad alive.

Throughout those ten days, surely the longest of my life, I could only watch his breathing, steady and deep, and listen to his cough, which became more and more ragged. But there were no more waking moments, only an occasional low moan or a facial contortion of discomfort, for which he was given small doses of morphine. I sat by his side, never forgetting that he had chosen to die. I totally understood and supported his decision. But it was excruciating to witness.

I confess there were moments I wanted to shake him awake, to give him sips of water, to put a touch of applesauce into his mouth, to rekindle his taste and love for food. But I couldn't. That would have violated his wishes and his desire to die sooner rather than later. Nevertheless, I wanted him to know how much I loved him and how I didn't want to lose him. Even in your weakened state, I wanted to tell him, you are precious to me and to all those who love you.

They say that the ability to hear is the very last of the senses to leave us. I hope and pray that John did hear me during those last awful days.

The day before he died, a Sunday, David drove down again. In the afternoon, a dear friend of ours, Jerry Anderson, an Episcopal priest, came by to see John. Together with other friends who were there as well, I asked Jerry whether he would be willing to offer us all, including John, Holy Communion. He agreed, and I went downstairs to the kitchen for a glass of red wine, which Jerry consecrated, and, as we all prayed together, I put a drop of the wine on John's tongue and Jerry gave him the Last Rites. He had no reaction, but I was so very thankful Jerry had been there on what became the last full day of John's life.

John Rehm died at 10:30 Monday morning, June 23, 2014. He died with only Musa at his side. I had spent Sunday night sleeping in two chairs next to him with our little dog, Maxie, on my stomach, fearing John might die without my being there to hold his hand. Early that morning, after Musa arrived, I gathered up my belongings and told him I was going home to shower, have breakfast, and return as quickly as I could. Sometime later, Dr. Fried arrived to check on how he was doing and called me at once to say he thought John was going to die within hours. I said I would be there as fast as I possibly could. But then Musa called, saying, "Diane, come quickly. I think John has just passed!"

By the time I got to his bedside, he was gone. All I could do was to weep over his still-warm body. Dr. Fried came to stand beside me, having left John just minutes earlier, when he was still breathing. His words of comfort, though thoughtful and caring, could not ease the pain, the choking realization that my beloved husband had finally, and with relief, passed from this life on to his next journey.

There was one last act, which at first I was reluctant to carry out. John's hand was closed into a loose fist, his gold wedding ring shining out at me. I caressed his hand, and, as I did so, Dr. Fried urged me to take the ring. I thought, I can't hurt his hand by unfolding it, but as soon as I tried, I realized his hand hadn't tightened, and I could easily slip the ring off. I now wear it on a gold chain around my neck, together with the diamond John gave me to celebrate our fortieth wedding anniversary.

Too soon, officials from George Washington University Medical Center arrived to carry him away. John and I had both decided to donate our bodies to medical science years before, when Jennifer was in medical school at Boston University. She had told us of the shortage of cadavers from which students could learn human anatomy, and so, hoping to make a contribution, we officially made the donation, just as John's mother had done when she died in 1990, at the age of ninety-two. A year later, a small wooden box containing her ashes came back to us, and several months after that, we spread her ashes beneath a huge hickory tree at our farm, the same tree beneath which John's father's ashes lie. John will join his mother and father under that beautiful tree, as will I, when my time comes.

I wanted to stay with him while the men from GW prepared to take him, but they gently urged me to leave the room. When they finally opened the door, I could see only the gray plastic shroud encasing him, something I'd never before seen other than on television or in movies. I put my arms around the center as he lay on the gurney and wept as I said a final goodbye to my beloved friend and partner.

David stood by my side as they wheeled John away. Then, together, we went back to my home to plan a memorial service.

⤳ Fifty-four Years of Marriage

When I think about our long marriage, my mind goes back to those early days when I as a secretary sat in an office at the Department of State, trying to make sense of this handsome and totally self-confident young man who was providing legal guidance to my boss about a U.S. trade agreement.

I could sense his curiosity about me, wondering why a young secretary should have such books as *The Brothers Karamazov*, the essays of Alfred North Whitehead, and *Of Human Bondage* on her desk. But there I sat, in my free time trying to educate myself about authors I realized other educated people had read. I wanted to know more about the world, and so I read.

I had had a wonderful high school education, but when graduation came, it was clear I would not be among the third of our class that went on to college. There were fundamentally two reasons: first, my parents couldn't afford to pay for such an extension of my education, and expected me to go to work as a secretary to help with the household expenses; and second, my parents, who had both immigrated to this country from the Middle East, did not believe higher education was warranted for a young woman. However, I was hungry for knowledge, most especially in the halls of the Department of State, where I felt inferior to those around me, people who were ambassadors, members of the hierarchy of the department, even clerks who had college degrees.

When he wasn't advising my boss, John began asking me

questions about what I was reading and why. What were my insights, what were my ideas, how did I interpret a certain essay or a particular character? And that interest in the books on my desk started a sweet flirtation between us. That he was interested in me was very flattering. I realized it was about more than just what I was reading.

Then we began to talk about baseball, which we both loved. At the time, I was playing second base for the State Department's women's softball team, while John pitched for the department's men's softball team. Our conversation, I recall so vividly, turned to that year's World Series, and we made a bet on which team would win. The bet: a dinner. He lost. I won. And we had our first dinner, which almost turned into a misadventure.

Without hesitation, John said he'd like to pay off the bet by taking me to what was then a Washington institution, Chez François. At the time, it was in the heart of our then relatively quiet city on Eighteenth Street, a beautiful and highly rated restaurant with a reputation for the finest French cuisine in town. And so we went by taxi, since neither of us owned a car at the time.

That dinner was one of the most memorable I've ever had. John and I never stopped talking, even as we ate and laughed and questioned each other about our current lives and backgrounds. I remember what I wore: a red silk blouse and a black velvet skirt. I recall the freshness of his smell, the beauty and strength of his hands, the elegance of his simply manicured nails, his blond crew cut, the kindness in his eyes. And yet at the end of the meal, I realized I was sick.

Perhaps out of sheer nervousness or due to rich food and wine to which I wasn't accustomed, I developed a terrible stomach-ache. As we left the restaurant, I told John I didn't feel well, and he suggested I come to his nearby apartment to rest before making the longer trip home. And so I did.

We walked into his modest efficiency apartment, where he suggested I lie down on his sofa. He then turned on his record player, putting on a recording of a piece of classical music. As I lay there, he sat quietly in a chair across the room, listening to the music with me. This went on for about an hour, until I felt my stomach easing and said I was ready to leave. He walked me to the curb and hailed a cab to take me home. And that was the glamorous end of our first date.

Happily, the first began a series of dates: dinner dates, walking dates, concert and theater dates, during which John became my teacher. There was no question I could ask him that he couldn't answer, whether it was about literature, music, foreign policy, or politics. He loved teaching me. He loved my questions. He told me early on that it felt as though I was the little sister he'd never had but always wanted. I can say with certainty that he rejoiced in my questions, in my curiosity, in my wanting to learn.

John was a born teacher, and confessed to me that, had it not been for the need to earn a good income, he would never have gone into law. He'd majored and excelled in Greek and Latin at Harvard, but in the end applied for law school, three years in his life that he did not enjoy. So I filled the student niche. His role as teacher, with me as pupil, continued for many, many years.

It was not until several weeks later that we kissed for the first time, in the boxwood gardens of George Mason's home at Gunston Hall in Virginia. Such a sweet and tender kiss. Perfect time. Perfect place.

After we were married, on December 19, 1959, student was not the only void I filled for John. To say that I craved friendship is putting it too strongly, but I did want to bring other people into our lives.

John's work at the State Department was regarded as brilliant. In fact, he was chosen by then legal adviser Abram Chayes as the youngest assistant legal adviser for economic affairs the State Department had ever had. In that position, he helped to create the Office of the U.S. Trade Representative (USTR) during the Kennedy administration. Then he became the first general counsel to that office, under Governor Christian Herter. John often said these thirteen years in government were the very best of his legal career. In fact, had Hubert Humphrey rather than Richard Nixon been elected in 1968, John might have stayed in government for many more years.

Since John's death, I have received several letters from his former colleagues, and none moved me more than this from Bernard Norwood:

> At the time we were in USTR, I was closer to no one than John. He was a warm friend, generous supporter, and great inspiration. Very soon after joining him in that office, I came to recognize, not only his great spirit and helpfulness, but also his special competence. His orderliness in thinking and drafting were striking. Rapidly and clearly, he put everything into its correct place—mentally and in writing. No "miscellaneous" file would ever be found in his file cabinet.

Those senior positions during both the Kennedy and Johnson administrations brought us many invitations to wonderful
events, which we both enjoyed. Further, we began to attend
St. Patrick's Episcopal Church regularly, which brought us into
contact with new people. We began to entertain, to cook for
large groups, many of whom have remained friends to this day.
John was a terrific host, always seemingly happy about having
parties and doing it all with good grace and humor. But not
necessarily with great enthusiasm. He would acknowledge that,
were it not for me, he probably would have led a more monastic
life, one where he spent most of his time alone, with music and
books.

John had such a brilliant mind, and he was a fabulous
listener—people loved being with him more than he loved
being with them. He adored talking with strangers, to learn
about their lives, to offer assistance when he could. And one
day, on a corner of Connecticut Avenue, he met an individual he
knew he had to do more than just listen to.

The man had set up a card table on which there was a single
sheet of written material, which he was trying to give to anyone
who would take it. Always curious, John stopped to read, and
began talking to Constantin Rauta, who poured out to him the
fact that he had been given asylum in the United States, but
that his wife, Kathy, and his infant son were being held by the
Ceauşescu government in Romania as punishment for Constantin's leaving the country.

Now I ask you, how many people would stop to listen, let
alone follow up on such a claim? But that's precisely what John
did. By this time, John had left government and was an attor-

ney in private practice. After doing a great deal of research on Constantin's claims, he went to Patricia Derian, then Assistant Secretary of State for Human Rights and Humanitarian Affairs during the Carter administration, and enlisted her help in getting Constantin's wife and son out of Romania. Months of pondering began over the best way to deal with the reality of the repressive regime in which Kathy was a virtual prisoner.

Finally, John himself went to Romania, purportedly to deal with a different legal problem. Secretly, he met with Kathy in a public park in Bucharest. She was very frightened, fearful even of John, afraid that somehow he was a secret Romanian agent sent to entrap her and put her in prison.

I was equally fearful of his going there, but John was determined. He knew he had to carry out this mission. He believed in Constantin, and believed he could be of critical assistance.

Finally, several months after that visit, due to John's efforts and with the ongoing help of the State Department, Kathy and her son were reunited with Constantin. Kathy's fears still lingered, but eventually she realized what John had done for her and her family, simply out of the goodness of his heart. He understood her fears and her reservations, and treated her with gentle kindness.

I will always remember John for that gentleness, whether it was toward another human being or a tiny spider. Whenever I spotted an insect in the house, John would find a way to capture the creature without hurting it, and deposit it outdoors. I admired his kindness and patience with others, even those I might be impatient with.

John was a loving man, a caring man, whom I adored for all

that he was and all that he gave to me, to his children, and to the world. I've said many times to myself and to others that were it not for John's love for me and mine for him, I might be dead by now. I realize that's a pretty dramatic statement, but it's true.

I was a smoker, from the time we met until after our second child, Jennie, was born, in 1964. I had started smoking when I was fifteen, and, by the time of her birth, I was smoking two packs a day. And one day John had the love and the courage to say to me, "The smell of cigarettes on you, on your clothes, in your hair, is not pleasant. I'm having a really hard time with it."

Vanity is a strong motivator. Several weeks later, at a New Year's Eve party we hosted, I stood up at midnight and told our guests I had smoked my last cigarette. John had doubts I would or could keep my word, but I just couldn't bear the thought that my husband was turned off by my scent. And so I never smoked another cigarette, and, today, I can thank my husband for helping me avoid what could well have been an extremely foreshortened life.

Throughout the early years of our marriage, I was basically content to be a homemaker, to prepare meals for our small family, to do all the necessary chores to keep a household running: the grocery shopping, the carpooling, the cooperative nursery school participation, and the entertaining. But John made two very important purchases for me that made a huge difference in my life.

First, a beautiful used baby grand piano. I'd wanted to study piano all through my childhood, but my parents could afford neither a piano nor lessons. And so I began taking piano lessons in my mid-twenties, satisfying my heart's yearning and feeling the gift of John's love as he perceived that yearning and found a way to satisfy it. Jennie and David followed on, both of them learning to play extraordinarily well, majoring in music in college. That same piano now sits here in my apartment.

Second, a brand-new Singer sewing machine. My mother had been a wonderful and creative seamstress, and I had taken basic sewing lessons in high school. I knew I wanted to try my hand at it again, and with John's wish to help me fulfill that desire, I began producing beautiful clothes, not only for myself but for the children, and even a few attempts at shirts for John, which he wore from time to time, perhaps more for my sake than because he really liked them.

And then came the fateful day when I accidentally and unknowingly found my new career. The year was 1973, and I was desperately seeking something to expand my horizons, knowing that soon my children would be completely out of the house and I would need to find some other way to feel useful in this world. By chance, a dear friend mentioned to me that she was enjoying herself immensely volunteering at a radio station on the campus of American University. Having been raised on radio, with all its wonderful soap operas and serials, and with no television in our home until I was fifteen years old, I was immediately intrigued. And so I asked whether she might introduce me to the person hosting the program on which she was working. A week later, my friend called and said I would be welcome to come for an interview. I was simultaneously thrilled and petrified, especially because of the location, American University. The fear of somehow being rejected because I was a non–college graduate rumbled in my stomach (where most of my anxieties seem to lie).

I found my future the very first day I walked through the doors of WAMU. At the time, it was a small radio station, not yet a member of NPR. I offered myself as a volunteer for a program called *The Home Show.*

From the start of those volunteer days at WAMU, John became my loudest cheerleader and greatest coach. He helped me deal with my fears, mostly about my own lack of knowledge and understanding of the world. He encouraged me, he brought me new ideas, he held me when I was overwhelmed, he loved me through all my doubts. And our love grew, as our children grew, even as we evolved into new people with new interests in the world.

Even after he moved to Brighton Gardens, John would offer ideas and suggestions for programs. He cared so much about life outside that room. Reading the *New York Times* and the *Washington Post* so early in the morning, he had always brought me new thoughts and insights that I could weave into my thinking about what ultimately became *The Diane Rehm Show.*

Our physical attraction to each other, so strong at the beginning of our relationship with that first kiss, endured long into our marriage. To say we "fit" perfectly is not an exaggeration. Together, we created a space for ourselves, something we both regarded as the most magical of all human miracles. Our greatest moments of openness came in those extraordinary expressions of love, when the receptiveness of two bodies allows for the sharing of minds. Together in those moments, we enjoyed the perfection of our marriage.

But no marriage is perfect, and certainly ours was far from it. I came to realize that John used lovemaking as a way to reconnect with me after a period of silence and distance. It was his way to avoid confronting the reality of *openly discussing* whatever the problem was. And it worked, because I was so hungry for reconnection that I rejoiced when the cloud lifted and we could once again speak to each other with warmth and kindness. Clearly, each of us would have become such a different person without the other. I know in my heart we were meant to be together, and, toward the end of his life, John acknowledged that as well. We were a team.

John comes to me now in short sentences, in words of encouragement, in moments of concern. And in the example he set for me and others throughout our lives.

⟿ The Memorial Service

Johan had indicated he would like the service to be held at St. Patrick's Episcopal Church, where he'd been baptized in 1979, at the age of forty-nine. We had attended services there for more than twenty years.

His had been a long journey toward Christianity, one he described vividly in his own book, *Onward Journey: Seeking the Divine:*

> *In the spring of 1979, I adopted the practice of dropping in at local churches at different hours. I would engage in an informal meditation, with no particular substance or direction. Something was at work within me, although my conscious being was puzzled.*
>
> *Then came June 23, 1979, a sparkling summer morning in Manhattan. I was walking up Fifth Avenue to have lunch with my mother near the Metropolitan Museum of Art. I came to 52nd Street and found myself spontaneously entering St. Thomas Church. I sat down in one of the pews. There were only a few other people in the church.*
>
> *The following events then took place in an extraordinarily rapid succession. I became aware of a Baroque air being rehearsed by an organist. The first line of Gerard Manley Hopkins' poem "The Windhover: To Christ our Lord" leaped to mind: "I caught this morning morning's minion, kingdom of daylight's dauphin, dapple-dawn-drawn Falcon. . . ." It was then blindingly clear that Christ had caught me, and His presence flooded every part of my being. He*

leveled the massive stone wall I had amassed against Him over the years. For a timeless duration, I sobbed uncontrollably in a paroxysm of joy. I left the church a new man and Christ's own.

Later that same year, John, whose parents had raised him without any belief in a Higher Power, was baptized as a child of Christ, with my dearest friend, Bishop Jane Dixon, acting as his godmother, and his law partner, David Busby, as godfather.

And now it was June 23, 2014. The symmetry was absolutely unmistakable: John died on the very same day, thirty-five years later, that he had felt the stones fall away and the light of Christ surround him in the Church of the Doubting Thomas. Many would say it was coincidence. I believe deep down that John felt himself moving toward a very special moment, a moment when he would actually be with God, and this became *his* day to go.

My first call when David and I got back to the apartment was to the rector of St. Patrick's, Reverend Kurt Gerhard, who had visited with John once several months earlier and given him Holy Communion. I wanted him to know that John had died, and to ask whether he, and St. Patrick's Church, would be available for a memorial service on Saturday, June 28. Kurt was in West Virginia that week, counseling young children at summer camp, but he readily agreed to hold the service on that date.

Then, with list in hand and David seated at the piano, the very piano John had given me so many years ago, we began discussing John's favorite hymns, relishing the beauty and memory of each one. Together, we narrowed the list down to about sixteen. David proceeded to play parts of each of them for me, and, as we sang together, the two of us agreed on those we felt could easily be sung by a congregation not wholly familiar with the hymnal.

Our friend David Dixon, Jane Dixon's widower, reminded us that Reverend Jim Holmes had come to know John when John began attending services of Holy Communion during the week. Jim came to my apartment a few days before the service and sat with David and me, going over aspects of John's life and outlook, which he then incorporated into his moving homily.

Hundreds of people attended the service. The flowers at the altar were utterly beautiful—John had often said he wanted no more "things" in life, just flowers. So many good friends and relatives and colleagues came to be with us, as well as several people I barely knew, whose lives had been touched by him.

As I heard people's comments that day about what John had meant to them and how his example had influenced them, I found myself wondering why we wait to say such important words to people we genuinely care for and admire. Why are we so reluctant to express our feelings of admiration and the importance our relationships play in our lives? Why do we wait until it's too late, when only survivors can hear those lovely words?

I admit that I, too, have failed on more occasions than I wish to remember to tell a friend how much she or he means to me. But for the past few years—and perhaps it is part of the aging process—I say to both family and good friends "I love you" before I put down the phone or watch them leave. Sadly, and this I've learned from experience, you never know when it will be the last time you have an opportunity to utter those words and have them heard.

After it was all over, after the music stopped and the reception line dwindled, after my children and their spouses and children had left, the apartment was empty, save for my twelve-year-old Chihuahua, Maxie, and me. I sat in the living room gazing at all the flowers sent by friends, trying to hold on to every detail of the beautiful service, but also wondering how John would have reacted, not only to the music and the words—especially to his son's reading from John's own book—but also to the outpouring of love and friendship that so many people offered.

They all had stories to tell or special memories to offer, some gesture John had made or word he had uttered that had stayed with them. John undoubtedly would have been surprised that so many people wanted to pay their respects, since he generally regarded himself as a man who needed and wanted virtually no one around him. But I was not surprised—John was a gentle, completely honest and decent man, whom everybody admired.

∽ *A Surprise Honor*

My Darling Scoop,[*]
    Just two days after your memorial service came a telephone call informing me that I had been chosen to receive a 2019 National Humanities Medal. My God, I thought, why couldn't this have come while you were still here to celebrate with me? I was sitting at my desk in my office, stunned after receiving the news, knowing how *you* would have let out a huge holler in delight. In my moment of "magical thinking," I almost picked up the phone to call Brighton Gardens to let you know.

You would so have loved all the ceremony that accompanied the event. First, a black-tie dinner at the Willard Hotel the night before the presentation at the White House. David came with me, representing you at a glittering dinner. Morgan Freeman, a man and actor I knew you admired and would have enjoyed meeting, was the emcee.

The next day, the actual awards ceremony began early, first with a gathering at the National Endowment for the Humanities. All of the ten Humanities honorees spoke to an auditorium filled with NEH employees, saying a bit about themselves and their accomplishments. I took those moments to speak of you and how, had it not been for your working to support the family and allowing me the opportunity to become first a volunteer and

---

[*]John's nickname from birth, Scoop, comes from his father's newspaper days in Paris.

then a radio talk-show host, this could never have come to pass. I felt your presence so strongly in that room.

Shortly thereafter we all boarded buses for the White House. Jennie and Benjamin had flown in from Boston just in time for the ceremony. Russell stayed in Boston with Sarah. David, of course, was there with Nancy.* Such a beautiful day and such a wonderful occasion, but you weren't there, laughing and celebrating each moment with our children and me.

When the time came for the actual presentation of awards, we were all seated in the East Room. As the Marine Band began to play ruffles and flourishes, everyone stood and the President of the United States and Mrs. Obama entered the room. What a thrill it would have been for you to meet the two of them.

Each medalist was called to the podium individually. When my turn came, I heard the citation read:

> To DIANE REHM, for illuminating the people and stories behind the headlines. In probing interviews with everyone from pundits to poets to Presidents, Ms. Rehm's keen insights and boundless curiosity have deepened our understanding of our culture and ourselves.

And then President Obama placed the medal attached to a red ribbon around my neck.

Afterward it was time for pictures. The Obamas were so generous with their time, taking photos not only with each of the ten Humanities and eleven Arts winners but with the families as

---

*Benjamin and Sarah are our grandchildren—the children of Jennie and her husband, Russell. Nancy is our daughter-in-law, David's wife.

well. A beautiful reception followed that reminded me so much
of the Christmas parties you and I used to attend at the White
House.

I missed you so much on that magical day, my darling Scoop.
If only you could have lived long enough to enjoy it. Then again,
knowing how you dreamed for me, I'll bet you were watching
the entire event from above.

∽ Guilt, Guilt, Guilt

I live alone now, in a condo high above the city of Washington, D.C., overlooking the changing beauty of Glover Park and the far-off landscape of Rosslyn, Virginia. Each clear night I watch the breathtaking sunset and wish that John were here with me to share it. I had never really lived alone. I had gone from my parents' home to a brief first marriage and then after a short time living with a roommate to marriage with John Rehm.

Washington has been experiencing one of its most glorious springtime displays in years. Everything is in bloom at once. The dogwoods, redbuds, azaleas, tulips, pansies: an extravaganza of color and beauty. Sometimes I sit on the steps leading to the garden of our condo breathing in the warm air and reflecting on my loss.

One of the first feelings that strikes me is Guilt, with a capital G. I've wrestled with my conscience and the conviction that I should have taken care of John myself during his final year and a half. But that would have meant giving up my career, and I wasn't ready to do that. And John wouldn't have wanted me to do that. Also, and it's hard to confess this, I recognize that some of us are caregivers and I suspect that I'm not one of them. That's not a comfort or even a justification, it's just the truth.

There are moments when the feelings of guilt are overwhelming. Here I sit in this lovely condo, in what was formerly John's bedroom, working at my computer in comfort, surrounded by beauty, peace, and privacy. John died in a bed in an assisted-living facility a few miles away, having all his physical needs taken care of by good people. But he was not in his own home.

Though John was in total agreement that the move to assisted living was necessary, that we lacked the ability to provide full-time care here in the condo, I am clearly responsible for his displacement and his discomfort. Had I said, "I will take care of you in this apartment," he might have stayed alive a little longer. But he had grown weaker and weaker, despite all efforts and medications. He was literally disappearing before my eyes. He seemed so sad, so vulnerable, unable to perform the simplest functions for himself.

Looking back, I ask myself whether I would have acted differently had our marriage been a more fully satisfying one. We had struggled through years of therapy, both individually and together, many times on the verge of divorce, only to realize, really to finally accept, how different we were as human beings. Might we (or I) have made a different decision regarding assisted living? Might I have moved heaven and earth to keep him with me, to live with him, take care of him, no matter what the sacrifice?

When I look back on our many years together, filled with both times of joy and years of hostility, the endless periods of silence, the physical and emotional distance between us, I realize it was almost inevitable that it had come to this.

In matters of companionship, John and I were total opposites. He grew up as an only child, completely doted on by his mother, playing alone as a toddler, learning to cope with parents who themselves had an extremely difficult relationship, and who lived apart for most of their married life. John often said he'd prefer to have lunch with *The New Yorker* than with any human being he knew. I realized that included me.

As for being with friends and attending social events, he agreed to do so only reluctantly, and managed to let me know just how uncomfortable it made him feel. Aside from his law partner of more than forty years, David Busby, he had no one he would ever phone or seek out to sit and talk with.

I, on the other hand, grew up surrounded by aunts, uncles, cousins, and family friends. There were so many evenings and Sunday afternoons when I would come home to find people visiting, seated in the living room with my mother and dad. Of course, they were all my father's relatives; my mother came to this country with no one, leaving behind her mother, sister, and brother, which was, I believe, a source of lifelong depression for her. Nevertheless, she enjoyed having visitors, and I loved seeing my many cousins and running off to play with them.

I'm fortunate to have many good friends, and lots of people I enjoy being with. Luckily, David Busby's wife, Mary Beth, and I developed a true and caring friendship during all the years our husbands were law partners. I talked to my dear friend Jane Dixon on the phone every single day for forty-five years, until she died. I had friends from high school with whom I kept in touch, and found myself open to enjoying new friends, something John was clearly reluctant to do.

Then, too, we approached our young children in totally different ways. John was far more popular as a parent than I was, in part because the kids could always go to him for a "second opinion" if I vetoed some activity or purchase. I was willing to engage with them, to take on the grief and anger that only children, and especially teenagers, can dole out. John was often the absent father, absorbed in his extremely important work during the Kennedy and Johnson administrations and, later, as an attorney in private practice. In reality, he was both adored from afar and in some ways resented by his children, as they witnessed the many terrible arguments we would have. Perhaps deep down they might have felt more comfortable had we parted.

As we grew older, even our tastes in food began to veer sharply apart. Whereas John had previously enjoyed my cooking, now he wanted little more than poached salmon, almost on a daily basis. Friends who invited us to dinner knew I would provide John with "special" food, or, generously, they would prepare it for him. I worried and fretted as he lost weight and grew increasingly thin and frail. If our lives together in times of good health had been so difficult, how could we possibly manage in illness?

For weeks, both of my children had been urging me to make the move—"The Move," as I thought of it—that would end the life together that John and I had known for fifty-three years. They saw, as I did, how difficult it had become to manage his health, his frailties, his tendency to do little more than sleep. They feared for him while I was out of the apartment, even for short periods. We engaged a caregiver for six hours each day, but there was still no way to ensure his safety.

But John resented having a caregiver with him while I was at work. He didn't believe he needed anyone, though, as time went on, the pain in his back (even after major surgery to insert rods and fuse discs) caused him to have to struggle to walk, bent over at the waist.

After a disaster with one caregiver who came to us through an agency ("I don't take people to doctor's appointments," she said. "I'm trained as a physical therapist!"), we luckily found Patience Adusei, a wonderful woman whose attitude perfectly suited her name. She was with us for nine months. Patience helped ease John out of bed each morning, stood by as he showered, helped him dress, and prepared his breakfast. She helped him navigate from his bedroom to the kitchen, where he could sit by the window and enjoy the *New York Times* while he ate.

After breakfast, she would rouse him, as he inevitably fell asleep after eating. He had been urged by his surgeon as well as his physical therapist to do leg and back exercises on his bed, but little by little the effort became more difficult. He could barely lift his legs or move his feet. Parkinson's was taking its toll.

And as time went on, he was sleeping more and more, and when he was awake he needed even more assistance with the daily chores of life. Sleep became his solace, his escape from a world in which he was increasingly losing control. Even his desire to attempt walking in our hallways was diminishing as the pain in his legs and back grew more and more severe. Ordinary remedies like Tylenol and Advil provided no relief, and any stronger medication brought on bouts of nausea and loss of appetite, something he really couldn't afford.

From the time he had been diagnosed with Parkinson's, five years earlier, he had lost nearly thirty pounds.

Finally came a night of physical hardship and utter sadness. John got up at 3:00 a.m. to use the bathroom, and fell. Though I didn't hear him fall, I awoke, sensing something was wrong, and found him lying on the floor in front of the bathroom, unable to get up.

I'd always heard that when people fall and can't get up by themselves it's nearly impossible to lift them. I tried anyway, with no success. John was like a 130-pound sack of rocks, willing but unable to help me help him. Somehow I managed to get him onto his knees, and then pull him to his bedside. Finally I got him up onto his bed. Just accomplishing this much took an entire hour. John immediately fell back asleep, exhausted from his efforts, while I, knowing my alarm would go off in less than an hour, sat wide awake, trying to consider the consequences of what we'd just been through.

When John woke up just as I was leaving for work that morning, he told me how sorry he was about what had happened. I understood how sad and embarrassed he felt. But I also knew that the time had come for us to have a serious talk about our future.

At dinner that evening, we were both very somber. John knew what I was about to say, and he knew that he would agree. The prior night's events had been the final wake-up call for both of us. We decided that I would begin looking at assisted-living facilities for him the very next day.

The fact that I went on working, plus John's always having been so careful about saving while *he* was working, is what allowed us even to consider the extraordinary expense of two separate residences. Assisted-living facilities are very expensive, even at their most basic. We were fortunate enough to find a residence for John close by, one that was the least institutional in appearance of any we visited.

Together we chose an apartment John liked, bright with sunshine, overlooking a combination of trees and cityscape, which, from its exterior, looked like an elegant condominium. And we created as homelike an atmosphere as possible, choosing drapery fabric identical to that in John's bedroom here at our apartment, and furniture that was simple but warm and inviting.

When the day arrived for John to move, in November 2012, Patience came to help me transport him. My husband offered no protest, no indication of regret or recrimination, no outward sign of sadness: pure John Rehm, who always had a chokehold on his emotions, never, through much of his life, allowing me or anyone else to know his internal struggles.

When I returned to our apartment at the end of that day, exhausted both physically and emotionally, I bowed to my enormous feelings of guilt and selfishness. It was as though I was standing in front of myself, screaming, "HOW COULD YOU?" And what could the answer be, other than "I had to. That's all there is to it. There was no other way."

I knew I would continue to feel the guilt, and would go on asking myself why I couldn't keep John here with me. I'm still asking myself: Why couldn't I have somehow made room for twenty-four-hour caregivers here at the apartment? Why couldn't I have given up my job to care for him? Why couldn't we have converted the apartment into a nursing care facility for John?

The guilt-laden questions are endless. I've gone over them with my children, my friends, my therapist, all of whom have been incredibly supportive of me and the decisions that John and I made. But I will never be able to completely erase that nagging feeling of guilt, nor will I ever be able to answer the *real* underlying question: Why weren't you willing to give up *your* life for *his*? Isn't that, after all, implicit in the marriage vows we took on December 19, 1959, and renewed twenty-five years later: "till death us do part"? Clearly, I was unwilling to give up for his sake the life we had both come to love, and in which he was no longer able to take part. I will always carry that guilt with me, even as I build a new life, on my own.

Now Maxie is my daily companion. He became an extraordinarily necessary one to John as well. I took him with me on every visit to John's living quarters, to be petted and adored by the man who had initially resisted having a dog.

*L*ike many women of my generation, I came into our marriage believing, and being totally comfortable with the idea, that my husband would take care of everything concerning finances. He would write the checks, he would pay the bills, he would oversee the savings needed for the children's college educations, he would take care of it all. Having John attend to the finances was a repeat of how my parents had operated. After all, I was *just* a homemaker, as my mother had been, caring for two young children. John was the one bringing in the income that allowed us to buy a home and put food on the table. In those early years, I never questioned his judgment about how the money was being used, because I trusted him completely. And he was *good* at it!

There did finally come a time, however, when I realized I needed to have a checking account of my own. I had become frustrated one day as I was shopping for a Christmas present for John. Finally, I found exactly what he'd asked for at a department store a few miles from home. I took out what I thought was a legitimate credit card, only to be told that the store no longer honored that particular card. I was furious. I had to return home, take a check from John's desktop checkbook (it was a joint account), and go all the way back to the store to purchase John's gift.

That night, I insisted to John that I wanted to create a checking account separate from his, one that would also be a joint account but would allow me to carry my own purse-size checkbook. John was furious, feeling somehow threatened by the idea that the checkbook in my hands would create a kind of independence for me that he neither anticipated nor wanted. It was the beginning of several weeks of silence between us.

When we finally managed to work out the division of financial responsibility, he continued to manage the "big" bills, like the mortgage, insurance, utilities, and savings, while I took over writing the checks for food, clothing, and miscellaneous household expenses.

By the time John retired from his law practice, in January 2001, he had spent five years planning for what would come next. He underwent a year's rigorous study and training so that he could serve as a volunteer docent at the Freer and Sackler Galleries of Asian art in Washington. He also became a volunteer at Reading for the Blind and Dyslexic, as well as a volunteer for the Washington Home & Community Hospices.

All went well for several years. We purchased a bright yellow Volkswagen Bug for him to travel around in, a car which suited him well and which he adored. And he loved his freedom, his independence, and his volunteer activities.

Then, beginning in 2005, came a series of automobile accidents, all within a period of eighteen months, each of them minor but nevertheless worrisome. After the third collision, John came home, pale and shaken, telling me he had hit a parked car on a side street near our home. Apparently, he had fallen asleep at the wheel. He was traveling slowly enough so that he wasn't hurt, and the damage to both cars was slight. However, three was the magic number for the insurance company to inform us they were canceling his insurance.

Hearing the news, John said simply, "Well, let's just find another insurance company." But I was worried and wary, and suggested that before trying to find another insurer we might do best to have him tested.

First, he was required to undergo a series of psychological exams at a nearby hospital, and, following that, he was given an actual driver's test with an evaluator. When he and the testing officer returned from taking the car out, the examiner said he would like to speak with me privately before talking with my husband. What he told me didn't surprise me. He said that he'd almost stopped the driving test after two minutes, since John was on the wrong side of the road as he tried to make a right-hand turn. He said that John's reflexes were no longer quick enough, that he had no clear sense of how to safely maneuver the car, and that it was his firm belief that John should no longer be driving. The tester, also a psychologist, indicated he found serious shortcomings in the results of John's tests for a man of his education. He asked how I felt John would react, and I replied that he would probably accept the facts without argument.

In fact, John said he was actually relieved, that he no longer enjoyed driving because it was creating too much anxiety for him. He knew he could rely on public transportation, and he was happy he hadn't harmed anyone while he had been at the wheel. The loss of the ability to drive was the first stage of John's gradual loss of independence, and the clear shifting of responsibility from him to me.

There were other disturbing changes in John that I began to perceive, primarily physical ones. For example, we would go for late afternoon walks together in the neighborhood, and I started hearing something different in his footfall. He, a man who had a posture and a stride I'd always admired, began to shuffle. He was not picking up and placing his feet on the ground as he had once done. When I asked him about it, he just shrugged his shoulders. It didn't seem to bother him, but it began to worry me. Also, there seemed to be much less movement of his arms, which previously had swung freely. A tremor developed in his hands, even as they rested in his lap. Putting these new behaviors together with the comments of the psychologist, we both felt it would be wise to seek professional help from a famed neurologist at Johns Hopkins University Medical Center, who had assisted in diagnosing me with spasmodic dysphonia back in 1998.

Dr. Stephen Reich is one of the most renowned specialists in Parkinson's disease and other neurological disorders. He had moved to the University of Maryland at Baltimore, and so, in late 2005, we made an appointment to see him. After a comprehensive physical and psychological examination, Dr. Reich concluded that John had symptoms of Parkinson's disease, a slowly progressing degenerative disorder of the nervous system. The disease, according to *The Merck Manual of Medical Information*, affects about one in every one hundred people over sixty-five years of age. John was seventy-five years old at the time of diagnosis. Dr. Reich prescribed levodopa and carbidopa, the primary drugs given to individuals with Parkinson's to help decrease the symptoms of the disease. They are sometimes given in combination with other drugs, which John tried to use, but which had significant and deleterious side effects.

Being given a diagnosis of a disease for which there is no cure, and which will inevitably worsen, is depressing, to say the least. In fact, depression is something many with Parkinson's experience. In addition, John's back was creating great problems for him, making it increasingly difficult for him to stand straight or even, at times, walk. In 2011, he opted to undergo back surgery which alleviated his pain for about a year. Eventually, however, severe pain returned in his back and legs and continued for the rest of his life.

Several months after we moved from our old home to our condominium, John brought me his checkbook and said, "I'm having trouble balancing this monthly statement. Can you help me?" I realized he had swallowed a great deal of pride to come to me with that request, and I was stunned. It had in fact been *he* who had taught me to balance a checkbook. But I simply said, "Sure." I managed to find the error in his calculations fairly quickly and handed him back his statement. I was worried but tried not to show it. He thanked me, and nothing more was said.

The very next month, however, the same problem occurred. I heard him muttering in frustration because he couldn't balance his checkbook. After I'd managed to put things in order, I heard words from him I would never have expected to hear. He said, "Maybe I'd better turn all the finances over to you. I seem to be having trouble keeping the simplest numbers straight." I looked at him and saw the sadness in his face, realizing what a powerful symbol of giving up this was for him. Thinking back, I recognize that we both wanted to weep.

∾ A New Model for Living

*B*eginning in that moment in 2011, John carefully briefed me on our total financial picture. I began paying all the bills, overseeing our savings, our investments, and our retirement plans. I realized that I actually had more ability in this area than I'd previously given myself credit for. The picture was complicated, but with John's initial assistance, I knew I could do it.

And of course, I *had* to do it! How fortunate that I had pushed back so many years earlier and demanded my own checking account. Otherwise I might have been left totally in the dark, as I know many women and men have been, about what is owned, what is owed, and how to treat the many obligations a family incurs.

Over the years I've heard from many people, especially women, who were absolutely stunned to finally realize the enormous number of obligations involved in operating a household. And who have had to face the financial secrets that one spouse may keep from the other, debts accumulated or separate accounts which have been kept private. I thank heaven that this was not true in our case.

There were many questions about our finances that John couldn't answer, however, so we called on our dear friend, John's former law partner and financial adviser, Bob Struyk. Bob had been the managing partner of the Minneapolis law firm Dorsey & Whitney when John and David Busby's firm merged with D & W.

Back in 1995, Bob had created a will for us and had mapped out a secure financial plan, assuming what we all assumed at the time would be our continued good health and well-being. He had remained our good friend and adviser, and now he came to Washington to help us sort through our future financial situation in the light of our newly revised outlook.

John and I had never taken out policies for long-term care, recognizing just how expensive they are, and that, should we need it, we could probably cover the cost ourselves. Now I realize that had we begun to carry long-term-care insurance in our fifties, while we were both healthy and in the workplace, we might have been better off.

And then we required new wills, and the naming of new trustees. On Bob's recommendation, we hired a new attorney to deal with the changes needed to ensure that our children would replace John and become executors of our estate when we were dead. A new financial overseer and investment adviser helped us on the best strategies to see us through both John's need for care and my need for continued subsistence.

The expenses associated with assisted living for John brought on many sleepless nights, but I knew that, as long as I went on working, I would be able to manage. Basic assisted-living costs for John added about $7,500 per month to our overall expenses. When he suffered pneumonia in March 2014, we hired a twelve-hour personal caregiver to be at his side during the day, at an additional cost of $1,200 per week. The agency that provided that special aide charged another $266 per week. All of which totaled more than $13,000 per month. Had John's savings and our investments toward retirement not been extensive, we would never have been able to afford this kind of care.

John's careful management of money during his working years came from having witnessed the lack of care with which his father managed money. Indeed, it was his mother who saved as much of their tiny income as she could, realizing that her husband was paying very little attention to providing security for their family. John grew up aware of his mother's concerns, and he told me of witnessing some of his parents' terrible arguments about his dad's carefree attitude.

I'm angered when I read about people who've lost their savings, their investments, even their homes, due to illness or natural disaster striking. Those who are supporting a family on minimum wage or Social Security or welfare, or who become homeless through no fault of their own, make me bow my head in sadness. Congress has done so much recently to affect the working poor negatively. And now, with the 2016 election process already under way, I fear there will be less and less assistance for those in need.

Up until John's diagnosis of Parkinson's disease, in 2005, we had both enjoyed good health. But the same is true of others who have crashed. John and I often talked about how lucky we were, shaking our heads and wondering why we should have been so blessed.

The Roller Coaster

Sometimes I feel as though I'm caught in an emotional land-slide. There are days I awake at 5:00 a.m., feeling I can't face the next moment. But I know I must get out of bed.

The week after John's memorial service, I knew I had to get back to work. *The Diane Rehm Show* had then been on the air for thirty-five years, and people relied on it. Listeners knew John had died, and many sent letters of comfort and condolence. I read each one, and was able to respond to many of them.

At first it was hard for me to concentrate. Having spent so much time each day worrying about John, I found it difficult to turn my mind completely to my work without memories of him and our life together distracting me. But work can be a balm, a salve for the soul of the mourner. I told myself not to forget that, and to remember that, no matter how successfully I was able to continue with the program and all it involved, I had to allow myself to mourn.

The grief comes in waves. I might be in the middle of an important on-air conversation on a subject involving, say, the Congress, while inwardly I am wishing John could hear it. And then I want to hear what *he* thinks about the subject, about the way government is or—for the most part right now—is not work-ing. My mind drifts. I feel that impulse to call Brighton Gardens to see how he is. I might be out on an errand and think, Oh, it's time to go see John. I wonder if it works this way for everyone.

Today, a lovely Sunday, I was out walking with Maxie when

I looked over to Maxie Park, which is what John and I used to call the spot to which John walked Maxie after we moved to our condo. He walked him three times a day while I was at work, loving every minute of it. We live near a sector of the city designated for community gardens, and they're constantly in bloom once spring comes.

Often, in the evenings or on weekends, we walked together through these gardens, talking over the events of the day. How I miss those walks and talks, holding hands, chatting with each other or with other dog owners. Our neighborhood is extremely well populated with dogs, and we inevitably encountered many people with dogs whose names we came to know. In fact, we knew the names of the dogs far sooner than we knew those of the owners!

Now Maxie has a dog walker who comes to pick him up every morning and returns for him at midday. But most evenings I'm home in time to walk him myself, and it's at those times that I can still see John with Maxie, talking with him, petting him, and making me wish I were there with them both.

❦ Our Bed

*L*ast night, for the very first time since I was married, I moved to the center of our bed. It's a queen-size four-poster, the bed John and I shared for many years, beginning when we first moved to our second home, on Worthington Drive in Bethesda, Maryland.

Up until now, and for all the years that John and I slept in separate rooms and then in separate residences, I've slept on "my" side of the bed. I couldn't manage to bring myself to sleep anywhere else. "His" side was his, with a pillow there for him. There was an emptiness, of course, on his side of the bed, but it never occurred to me to shift and assume possession of the entire bed: always, his presence was there in my mind, head on pillow, turned either toward or away from me. But last night, nine days after his memorial service, I hesitantly decided to move my pillows to the center. I knew I would feel awkward, but I wanted to try. I spent the entire night wide awake, unable to shake the finality of the shift and what it represented.

Shortly after John and I were married, in 1959, we bought a lovely two-bedroom house, and we moved into it when I came home from the hospital with our newborn son, David, in my arms. The bed we slept in was a double, barely big enough for two adults, but we had no complaints; as a newly married couple, we were happy to share the space. When David was an infant, we frequently brought him into our bed, to watch him feed, sleep, and smile. Then Jennifer came along, and by the time she was three, it was time to look for another home.

The house we found on Worthington Drive afforded more space for each of us. David and Jennifer could have their own rooms, John could have a study, I could have a sewing room, and in our bedroom we could finally have a lovely queen-size bed.

The bed has always been such a powerful symbol—of beauty, of love, of hostility, of anger, and of peace. I think of our bed in all those ways during our fifty-four years together, times when we were madly in love and physically enjoying each other; times when we were watching a television program together before sleep, laughing or commenting about what we were seeing; times of silence, when we weren't speaking to each other, yet continuing to share the bed; times when one of us was sick and the other became the nurse-caregiver; and finally, the time when I moved to another room, because John had developed myoclonic movements affecting his entire body, causing him to jump slightly every few seconds. I'm a light sleeper, and, as a result, we decided I would move into what had been Jennifer's room, since by then she had left for college.

I look back on sharing our bed as one of the most important elements of our life together. So much joy, so much fun, laughter, happiness, and physical warmth. Perhaps that is why I've been so reluctant all these years to move to the center of the bed. I've said to others, since John's death, "I'll be okay. I've been by myself for a long time." But I realize it's not completely true. Of course I can carry on, and I shall. My work is vastly important to me, and thank God I have it. I will go on rising at

5:00 a.m. daily and preparing for the day ahead. I will shower, have breakfast, dress, put on my makeup, take care of Maxie, get into my car, and drive to the WAMU studio.

But I am grieving. I realize I want to be by myself, with my memories and my tears. I don't want to be in the company of others, even good friends, who are laughing and sharing ideas and stories. I'm reluctant to go downstairs to the lobby of my condo for mail, afraid I'll run into a resident with whom I'll have to exchange pleasantries, and even respond to condolences.

Instead, I want to reach for the phone. I want to tell John how I'm feeling, and how much I miss him. Only he can truly understand. As he lay there in his own bed at Brighton Gardens, hardly moving, still breathing but no longer speaking, his essence remained. Even as he lay there dying, I knew I could tell him what I was feeling and that he would express support and love.

Some months before John died, I climbed into his narrow bed with him, put my arm around him, and read to him. At first, he'd asked for Thomas Hardy's *Jude the Obscure.* After several days of half-hour readings, he said he'd prefer short poems, and so I brought him a book of haiku, which he loved. We held hands in his bed as I read to him, and kissed each other with great tenderness. I shall cherish those moments forever, because somehow, with the two of us in his narrow hospital bed, with aides walking in to give medication or offer a menu, smiling as they saw us, we were closer in spirit than perhaps we'd ever been. And now I sleep in a queen-size bed, pillows in the center, alone.

ᴖ I Think I'm Okay

Today is Saturday, a day I look forward to all week because I can sleep later than 5:00 a.m. But this morning I frantically woke myself at 7:45, having experienced one of the most horrific dreams I've ever had in my life.

In the dream, John and I are at the farm with David and Jennie. We go for a walk, all together, crossing beautiful fields, looking at Queen Anne's lace, yellow cornflowers, and cattails. As we cross a hill we come upon three Native Americans, dressed in full Indian garb, with feathered headdresses and bows and arrows strapped across their backs.

In my dream, I've never before come face-to-face with a Native American, especially not there in the farm hills, but since they are *there,* I assume they're friendly.

In the next moments of my dream, I realize how wrong I am. I see that John has been murdered, along with Jennie. They are both lying facedown, wrapped in multicolored blankets, with arrows coming through the blankets extending from their backs.

I say to David, "RUN!" He and I run as fast as we can. But David, apparently trying to cover my retreat, runs behind me even though he can run much faster than I. Then I hear the heart-wrenching sounds of his being caught and slaughtered.

I keep running as fast as I can, knowing that I will certainly be the next to die. The Indian is running fast behind me, reaching for me, telling me I must drink something he's carrying. I know it's lye or something else equally deadly, because I remember—

in my dream—having seen a home break-in where the murderers pour lye down the throats of their victims.

I keep running, running, running, until finally I enter a cave. And then I see an opening in the ground, almost large enough for me to crawl into, but I realize there is brown roiling water at the bottom of the opening. I stand there, knowing if I don't go into the opening, I'll be caught and will die by the most unbearably painful poison.

I force myself to wake. I am shaking. At first I'm totally baffled by what seems such a bizarre dream. Why? But as I lie there, trying hard to recall every detail before it drifts away, the details become less important than the overall feeling I'm left with: fear. The fear of being left alone. There is no one to protect me. I am alone, by myself, with total responsibility for myself. John is gone, and my dream reminds me to acknowledge how his no longer being on this earth makes me feel. I *say* I'm okay, to everyone who asks. And outwardly, I am. But there is clearly that part of me, deep down, going all the way back to childhood, that remains afraid of being left alone.

∽ Sunsets

John always said it's *after* the sunset that the magnificence appears, the colors glow, the light changes.

I watched the sun go down tonight shortly after 8:00 p.m. I watched the golden globe as it dropped behind the distant line of trees that form the horizon from my fourteenth-story window. I watched it until it disappeared, the last tiny shimmer vanishing. And then came the glow. The pinks, the grays, the mauves, the streaks, the whiffs of clouds. All so delicate and so beautiful. Maybe John was seeing ahead, to a time when he would no longer be with me, when he agreed to buy this beautiful apartment.

Today I cried all the way to work in the car, talking to him as I went, wondering whether he was with his mother and father, whom he adored; whether he saw them whole or in spirit; and whether he had met *my* mother and father, who were both gone long before I even met John. I always felt that once they got to know him they would have loved him. He would have been a stranger to them, so bright, seemingly so confident, so articulate, when in reality he suffered so many of the same doubts about himself that I did about myself.

This morning, Lisa Dunn, one of my producers, asked me in a quiet moment, "Are you okay?" Well, not really. I'm so sad. And then I told another producer, Susan Casey, how hard it is not to have someone to share the day-to-day occurrences with, just the simple "Well, I feel sad today." And John would say,

"What's it all about?" And then he would help me sort through my sadness.

Sometimes, when something good had happened in my life, he would say something to the effect of "You know, whenever you've had some wonderful honor or compliment, something in you tells you that you don't deserve it. Is that what's going on now?" I can hear his voice. I can feel him next to me, asking that very question. And I think he was right back then, and he's right now.

⤳ The Long Glide

My life alone began long before John died. When he moved to Brighton Gardens, in November 2012, he had hoped that he would someday return to our condominium, but I knew this was not realistic.

Walking back into this apartment for the first time, knowing he was not here and likely would not be here again, filled me with extreme apprehension, as well as—and I have to acknowledge it—a sense of relief. Relief because I knew that someone else would now have the responsibility of caring for him, of watching out for him, holding him upright, serving his food, answering his every need, nor would I have to worry each time I walked out of the apartment heading for the office that he might fall or leave the gas stove on while I was gone.

The apprehension was far greater than the relief, however. Now my responsibility had broadened, extended to caring from afar for another human being, as well as taking care of all my own needs, professional, personal, and financial.

Yet I think for me the greatest apprehension was, How do I live alone? How do I start navigating the world from a changed perspective, that of living without a spouse? Living without someone to say "Good morning" to, someone who would ask me, "How are you, and how did you sleep last night?" Such tiny words, gestures, taken for granted between husband and wife, and now, in one single day, gone.

Of course I could talk with John on the phone every day,

share with him what was happening in my work or in the world around us. And at first he was reading the *New York Times* each morning, trying to keep up with the news. We purchased a large television set for his room, so he could watch news or entertainment programs, but little by little, his interest in what was happening in the world left him.

Returning home each evening, either directly from work or from Brighton Gardens, I immediately turned on my radio or the television. The sounds of the human voice are so incredibly important to me. It's hard for me to be in a completely silent atmosphere.

I feel alone.

I wish my children and grandchildren were nearby. Their presence on a regular basis would no doubt have made the transition from John in the apartment to John at Brighton Gardens easier to endure. As it was, David tried to make it down from Gettysburg at least once a month, sometimes more frequently, always to visit John and then have an early dinner with me before returning home.

Jennie and her husband, Russell, both incredibly busy physicians and the parents of two young children, had very little time during that year to be with us, although the entire family was able to come to Washington for Easter Sunday 2014. Along with a few close friends, we prepared an Easter brunch to take to Brighton Gardens. That day allowed Benjamin and Sarah to see their grandfather for what would be the last time.

Our children have very full lives, and I can't expect to fit into their schedules, nor would I really want to. Of course I would love it if they were nearby and our nearness became the natural way of things, with an occasional drop-in visit, but that is not likely to be. I admire their independence, their stability, and their ability to take charge of their own lives, and certainly don't expect them to take on the responsibility of keeping *me* happy.

All this became clearer and clearer to me from November 2012 to the day John died. I knew I was on my own. But I still had the benefit of having John with me, even though he wasn't physically present. I think of those spouses whose husbands or wives have died completely unexpectedly, rather than after long illnesses. How do they manage? How do they adjust?

Looking back, I find myself wondering how different grieving may be when one loses a loved one suddenly, with no preparation, no signal of illness, no worry of impending loss. Is it more difficult to wake up after just weeks rather than months or years and realize you've lost the partner with whom you've shared a lifetime? Are there regrets at not having had time to say what you might have wanted to say? Is there greater sadness that lingers longer?

Joan Didion writes vividly about the sudden death of her husband, John Gregory Dunne, in her book *The Year of Magical Thinking*. He suffered "a sudden massive coronary event" on December 30, 2003. While she was preparing dinner, he sat in his favorite chair, drinking a Scotch and talking. She writes, "John was talking, then he wasn't." Shortly after the emergency medics got him to the hospital, a social worker broke the news to her that her husband had died. At the time, she writes, she remembers thinking, "I needed to discuss this with John. There was nothing I did not discuss with John."

She recounts in poignant detail the sense of near madness

she experienced during that first year after his death, exploring, as she puts it, "the power of grief to derange the mind." She came onto my program to talk about the book, and a more frail and fragile creature I don't believe I've ever encountered. Sudden death of one so close is devastating, as she so powerfully shared with my audience.

My dear friends Roger and E. J. Mudd had been married for fifty-four years. He had long before retired from his estimable career in radio and television with CBS, NBC, and PBS. The four of us had traveled together to Italy, where Roger navigated the winding roads and E.J., with her wonderful knowledge of the language, had no hesitation approaching residents to ask directions, and with her warm and genuine manner elicited recommendations of restaurants that they themselves enjoyed. E.J. was strong and healthy, with only the minor maladies that accompany the aging process. There was always a beautiful glow in her face.

Early one morning several years ago, E.J. awoke and called out to Roger, "I think I'm having a heart attack." Within minutes, an ambulance arrived to take her to the hospital. As she was about to be transported, the very last words she spoke to Roger were "I don't want to do this." To this day, Roger is not sure whether she meant she didn't want to go to the hospital or she didn't want to die.

She was immediately put into intensive care with a breathing tube blocking her ability to speak. When she tried to communicate by pencil and paper, E.J., the spectacular writer of essays and poetry, could no longer make her writing decipherable. Ever the optimist, Roger had no sense that she was facing death, and was thinking about acquiring a walker for her when she was ready to leave the hospital. Every night he wrote bulletins to family and friends, filling us all in on E.J.'s condition. Only after she'd been in intensive care for more than a week did he begin to realize that she might not live. He recalled a poem she'd written in which she'd said that, even when death relieves pain, it's sad to die and leave one's place in this beautiful world.

She died nearly three weeks later, with her husband and four children by her side.

The shock of E.J.'s death is still with Roger, after more than three years. He's getting used to the lack of her physical presence but has remained—alone—in the big old farmhouse they shared for many years. Staying in the house has made it easier, he says, because her presence is all around him. He describes their marriage as a "knockout" because they had such respect for each other.

Sometimes he remembers things he meant to tell her, and the hardest part is missing those moments of intimacy, when they would confide in no one but each other.

Roger says he's not sure he wants the sadness to get easier, because he fears that would mean that the memory of their wonderful life together would begin to fade. He has described moments of grief so intense that all he can do is lie on E.J.'s bed and weep for an hour or so. But psychologically, he says, he does not truly realize—or accept—that she's gone. When he's sitting on their front porch, looking out after dinner on the beautiful sloping green landscape, as they did together for so many years, his eyes fill with tears.

Eleanor Clift and her late husband, Tom Brazaitis, went

through a seemingly endless period of suffering. In 1999 Tom had had one cancerous kidney removed and was told that, since the cancer was contained, he would enjoy a complete recovery. However, that was not to be. A year later, the kidney cancer had metastasized to his lung. Tom took complete charge of his disease, researching it thoroughly before undergoing a series of debilitating chemo and radiation treatments, all of which left him unbearably weak and with horrible bouts of chills, nausea, and pain. He wrote of his experience in columns for his newspaper, the *Cleveland Plain Dealer*.

When he was no longer able to manage stairs, his bed was moved to the living room on the first floor, where he had access to both bathroom and kitchen. Over a span of months, this once strong and vital man deteriorated, with Eleanor helping with his care and feeding even as she continued her work with *Newsweek* and the weekly television program *The McLaughlin Group*. Since John was working at the time as a hospice volunteer, Tom asked him to visit, which John did on a weekly basis, sometimes reading to Tom, other times quietly sitting with him.

When Tom finally died, in 2005, it was a blessed relief. But did the preparation Eleanor had experienced by watching Tom decline physically and emotionally help to ease the loss? Or was her sense of loss and mourning the same as Roger Mudd's? Or Joan Didion's? How *does* one compare experiences of grief?

When I spoke with Eleanor, she described the huge hole Tom's death left in her life. But, she said, "I ran away from grief as fast and hard as I could." She jogged, she worked, she accepted invitations. Attending a support group for other grieving people made her feel worse. People would say to her,

"You're so *strong!*" And her response was "How else can I be? I just keep on going." Eleanor confessed that continuing with her routine during Tom's illness had given her a sense of control in the midst of watching her married life fall apart.

Is there a difference in the extent of the blow to the body and psyche of the survivor if there has been time to adjust to the loss beforehand? A dear friend, Jeff Stann, wrote to me recently. His wife, Patsy, died in 2011, having been diagnosed with lung cancer four years earlier. He wrote that some months after that diagnosis, he realized he had already entered the "grieving process." He found himself sitting at a stoplight sobbing, something he said happened throughout the years of her illness and still recurs occasionally at times when he's alone. Recently, he said, he went to the drugstore to buy some bandages. "Standing in the aisle looking at the two-by-two- and four-by-four-gauge sponges and the other paraphernalia of wound healing, I could feel the memories coming back of buying all the same products for Patsy three, four, five years ago. A sad moment, and I was happy the aisle was free of other patrons."

Jeff is a hiker, and he says the Appalachian Trail has been central to his grieving. "I've always regarded the outdoors as a kind of cathedral space in which to imagine and address the divine. And when you are walking alone for hours and days on end, your mind can approach and surround a subject without interruption."

I think back to my mother's dying. I was just fifteen, and was visiting our family doctor because of an ear infection. I'd been worried about my mother, who'd been in and out of the hospital for the past several months, but no one would tell me what was happening. So I asked the doctor, directly, "How is my mother?" And he answered, equally directly—and to my mind, brutally— "Your mother has no more than a year to eighteen months to live." No reasons given, just the reality of one doctor's diagnosis.

My mother actually lived for four more years, dying when I was nineteen, with a diagnosis that still makes no sense to me. We were told it was cirrhosis of the liver—this for a woman who, at most, had two shot glasses of whiskey each year: one at Christmas and one on New Year's Eve, sharing a toast with my father. If it was, indeed, cirrhosis, perhaps it was the result of a blood transfusion she'd had many years earlier after her gall-bladder was removed, or of some other undiagnosed infection.

The exact cause of her death is perhaps of no matter all these years later, except for the fact that, with today's medical advances, she might have had a liver transplant, given that she was so young when she died, just forty-nine. I think now of her long suffering, how in the last weeks of her life in the hospital she begged for no more treatments, no more draining of the fluids that left her stomach so distended, no more invasions of her body.

On the last full night of her life, New Year's Eve 1955, I went to see her, but she was barely awake. When the knock on the door of my apartment came the next day, I rushed to the hospital, but—as I've already written—as with John, I got there a few minutes too late. First as a fifteen-year-old, then as a nineteen-year-old, I knew death was coming to my mother. Did knowing throughout the four years between the two dates help to ease the pain of loss when it finally came? Did the awareness make it easier for me to accept and move on? The answers to those questions are resounding *noes*.

My father suffered a massive heart attack eleven months later. The doctors assured us he'd be fine, but that same night at 1:00 a.m., I received a call from the hospital saying he had died. To my mind, his heart was literally broken at the loss of his beloved Eugenie.

To this day—and as I write I am seventy-eight years old—I grieve the loss of my parents, most especially my mother. I never got to know who she was, never understood her sadness, never realized the losses she had experienced, never grasped why we had such a difficult relationship. I grieve the lack of understanding between us.

I grieve for my adulthood without her, believing that if only she had lived and I'd had the chance to ask her about her life not only here in this country but with her family back in Alexandria, Egypt, I could have begun to understand her better. As it is, I will forever grieve losing her.

But does any human being *really* know another? John was so internally focused that it was enormously hard for him to share himself, with me or anyone else. One moment I would think I truly understood him, the next he would do or say something that would force me to reevaluate. Still, I'm grateful that, as his life was drawing to an end, he wanted to express his regret to me for the many moments, hours, months, even years, of emotional hardship we'd endured. It was a moment of clarity, and certainly a relief for both of us. Yet exactly what motivated him at that very moment, why he spoke out, he was never able to explain.

Had John died suddenly, would I wonder forever, as I have with my mother, why our lives together couldn't have been easier? Would I have gone on blaming myself for not having been the right woman for him? I must confess that I still think in those terms. Had the woman he married been more passive, happy to be led, more submissive (as clearly I was at the beginning of our marriage), would John have been a happier husband? I'll never know.

I do realize just how needy I was, first as a young wife and mother, and later on, too, looking for emotional support. I craved attention, and perhaps the more I expressed that need, the more defensive and distant John became. He, after all, had his own career, his own burdens of responsibility. He supported our family through my years of nonworking, volunteer work, and finally modest salaried employment. He bore the financial burden and perhaps had to protect himself from the burden of years of my neediness.

In fact, in July 1987, I wrote a letter to a dear friend who had gone to a clinic in Florida for food addiction treatment. I came across that letter recently, going back through a journal I kept for almost thirty years. Here is what I wrote:

> *The whole idea of addiction fascinates me, not only as it relates to food and alcohol, but as it relates, in my case, to a relationship. I'm only beginning to get a glimmer of the reality that is my addiction, but I can describe it as a fear, a basic insecurity, that comes over me when I imagine myself without that relationship, i.e., my marriage. It's as though I have to constantly quiet the internal hunger*

*for closeness, for affirmation, for love, for acceptance, which I don't
seem able to supply to myself. In much the same way that perhaps
you feed yourself with food, I feed myself with constant thoughts
and fears which, in a strange way, eat away at me, so that the only
way I can be nourished is by the constant reaffirmation that Scoop
loves me and won't abandon me. The fear of abandonment is so
overwhelming that I drive myself deeper and deeper into depression, knowing there is no internal resource with which to comfort
and succor myself. It has to come from him and that has been my
sickness.*

*All this is by way of saying that you're the one at the treatment
center for what is an externally visible addictive disorder. I'm the
one sitting at this typewriter, who, at least by external signs, would
be judged a non-addictive personality. But I know that's not true.
My ongoing struggle is to quiet the non-visible demons that drive
me—not to food or drink, but to self-doubt and hunger for other's
(Scoop's) adoration. I can't have it, and I have to learn to be a big
girl and find the love and acceptance within myself. What I'm trying
to say (and doing a lousy job of) is that your willingness to confront
yourself is inspiring to me, and I am trying, minute by minute, to
confront the reality of my own addictive behavior. Change is probably a long way down the line. Someday I'll even have the courage to
say all this out loud, and that will be a big step forward.*

And in fact, that's what I am at last doing now. When John's
illness began and I realized we had to concentrate more on *his*
physical and emotional state of being, our relationship began
to change rather dramatically, into a softer, more mutually sup-

portive engagement. I went with him to every doctor's appointment, helping to clarify, for both of us, what we were hearing and how his illness might evolve. We shared with each doctor how Parkinson's disease was affecting his walk, his movement, his alertness, his appetite. We understood—together—that there were few options, and that the way forward would not be easy. But we were together, perhaps in sickness even more than in health.

∼ Sickness

Throughout our long marriage, when one of us was sick, the other fell into the role of good nurse. John's comfort with that role went back to his childhood when he and his mother were living alone in New York City and she came home from the hospital after a hysterectomy. At this time his dad was back in Europe carrying out aid operations for the government. John completely took over running the household. It was during World War II, so there were rationing stamps to be dealt with, food preparation, dishwashing, and the cleaning of their tiny apartment. John learned how to care for his mother and, subsequently, me.

Whenever I was ill with a bad cold or flu, or after two surgeries, he was a wonderful nurse to me. In fact, early on in our marriage, when I was in the first months of pregnancy with David and forced to bed rest, John left his job at the Department of State every day to come home to prepare lunch for me so I wouldn't have to use the stairs. Later on in our marriage, after he had the first of two major back surgeries, we had dinner in our bedroom every night after I returned from work, meals I came home to prepare and take to him. Those moments are very special in my memory. Of course we both knew that he would get better eventually, that each day as he grew stronger the long siege was coming closer to its end. And that made all the difference. It was a very different outlook from the one that faced us with John's Parkinson's disease, which slowly but surely robbed him of everything that made him feel useful in this world.

So now I wonder: Who will take care of me when I get sick? Who will cook for me? Who will sit by my bedside? I try not to dwell on these thoughts, instead relying on my awareness of my good health and strength. Yet the feelings creep in. What if I were to fall again as I did five years ago, when I broke my pelvis? What if I were, again, in the hospital for three weeks? How would I manage? The what-ifs are endless.

Those what-ifs include fear of a stroke, or of Alzheimer's. So many people I know have suffered from some form of dementia and lost the ability to care for themselves. Those are my greatest fears. I pray that I go suddenly, quickly, and of course without pain. But how many of us are lucky enough to experience that kind of death?

I want to be prepared. I want to know I can be in control of my own life and, indeed, my own death. Of course all is in the hands of God—I believe that—but I can't help wishing I won't be burdening my family with a long, debilitating decline.

The other night I invited a few women friends over to watch the 2015 Super Bowl. Each of us had prepared food to enjoy while watching the game. But before it began, I told them I could offer them another option: I had a screener of the movie *Still Alice*, based on the novel by Lisa Genova. Without hesitation they all said they'd rather see the movie.

I don't think I'm alone in worrying about whether I'll find myself experiencing the same plight as the heroine of that novel and movie. She is a brilliant Harvard psychologist who begins forgetting—small things, at first: words, phrases, directions—

until ultimately she finds herself lost in neighborhoods that she's known for decades. It's all downhill from there. I'm certain that each one of us watching that film was saying to herself, Please, God, not me.

My children, as I've said, have their own lives. My beloved closest friend, Jane Dixon, is gone. I have many good and even "close" friends, but naturally they all have their own lives and their own frailties.

The Team of Rehm is no longer. I was once half of a complete team, and although the other half of the team was frail over the past few years, my half was strong. Now I'm on my own. How will I make preparations for serious illness? Legally, financially, I think I've done all I can. But emotionally? It's a fear I have, and one about which I've begun to think seriously. Like John, I don't wish to suffer endlessly without hope of return to a normal life. Preparation is the only answer.

M y Dearest Love,
     I'm so tired tonight. It's been more than nine months
now since you've been gone. If you were here and I'd come
home feeling and looking as I do right now, you'd be urging me
to slow down and take better care of myself, to eat more (you
don't like it that I've lost twenty pounds), to get to bed early.
You'd tell me to get into bed, and then you'd bring me a glass of
champagne.

The world is such an awful place right now. In some ways I'm
glad you're not here to witness the horror of what people are
inflicting on themselves and on others. I'm so afraid that America may be drawn into yet another terrible foreign war, with the
loss of many lives, and even the threat to civilians in this country.

You're not here, smiling as I leave the apartment, helping me
to get through each day when I have to go on the air, to deal with
questions, to be strong, to be fair, and to try to transfer the belief
you've always had in me to this wide audience that has come to
rely on me. Yes, I'm feeling sorry for myself, and I really have no
right to. I grieve, my darling husband, I grieve.

Losing you is so hard. I'm alone, as I never expected to
be. Your mother lived until she was ninety-two years old, so I
assumed that you had longevity on your side. But she had a very
bad hip and lots of pain, having refused surgery. We both knew
that someday she would take her own life, and she did. Your
father died at seventy-two, suffering from diabetic retinopathy.

His life became impossible for him, living alone at his farm, so he, too, took his own life.

And now you. You decided it was time for you to die. I will always wonder whether you did it, really, because you didn't want to live any longer, or whether you decided you wanted to spare your family the difficult long-term consequences of your staying alive, watching you lose more and more of your ability to speak, to care for yourself, to think and reason. Was it for you, or was it for us? I should have asked you that.

Instead, I accepted your decisions because they were your stated wishes. I didn't feel I could interfere. Should I have? Should I have begged you to stay alive? Should I have said to you, "It doesn't matter, just keep going! Whatever your condition, we'll be here for you."

But I didn't try to change your mind. And I will forever question *my* decision.

I know I have no right to feel self-pity. I am healthy, I have work to keep me busy, I live comfortably. But the loss of you has been so hard. I want to bring back the memories of times when you and I were here together, working on Christmas cards or finances or e-mailing your book editor, or just talking. You taught me so much about patience and tolerance and perseverance. You educated me about so many things—literature, art, the world I didn't know until you. I want to hold on to every one of those memories.

I love you, my darling Scoop. I hope you can hear/see/know that.

↜ Heaven

One day as John and I sat together in his room at Brighton Gardens, it began to rain. We both love rain. In fact, when I was a child, my mother and I used to sit together on the sofa in our small den with our faces turned toward the window, watching the raindrops fall. It's one of my special memories of being with her. John said, "I wonder whether there'll be raindrops in heaven. I'd miss the rain." And before I could say anything in response, he said, "Perhaps they'll be bigger raindrops." We both smiled.

I'd like to think there is a heaven. When I asked Roger Mudd whether he believed in heaven, his answer was yes. "What does heaven mean to you?" I asked. "An absence of pain and suffering," he responded. That answer appeals to me, but I want to believe there is more. I want somehow to visualize something, however nebulous. I want to believe in the reports of those who say they've experienced some form of heaven, whether it's "the light" or a "presence" beckoning them. But I think my own idea of heaven goes beyond that. I want to believe that my husband has been reunited with his parents, has met my parents, and is with Jane, his godmother, who adored him. I still hear her laughing, amused at some outrageous statement or action of mine. She would be so welcoming to John, greeting him with open arms, and he would feel totally comfortable and happy in her presence. E. J. Mudd, always so kind and solicitous of John, is there to shine a sweet smile his way, understanding his decision to end his life, ready to help him begin a new "life," in the arms of God.

My dear friend Mary Beth Busby wrote an e-mail to me one day when I was feeling particularly down. She said, "I have no clue as to whether or not there is a heaven, but I believe in it because it makes *me* happy to imagine a continued relationship now—and a reunion later on—with those I have loved. And your Scoopy is right up there."

My own belief, I realize, is rather childlike: they—all of my beloved relatives and friends now gone from me—are with John, and he is refreshed, he is new, he sparkles in their presence. He is without illness, as they are, and somehow each of them is engaged with all the others. Heaven, in my mind, has no bodily presence, only spiritual. And it is through the spirit that my loved ones are connected with each other. Do they see us? Do they know what is happening here in what many refer to as the "real" world?

I have always felt such strong connections to my parents, now gone more than half a century, that I can't help feeling (again, that word *feel*) the same about my husband. He is with me still, he's by my side, encouraging me to face my fears, reminding me of how strong I am, watching over me, letting me know each day, in the music I hear, in the flowers I tend on the balcony, in the raindrops I feel on my face, that he is with me. Is that what heaven means? That's what heaven means to me.

Recently I watched the movie *Heaven Is for Real,* the story of a four-year-old boy, the son of a Nebraska Wesleyan Church pastor, who, while undergoing emergency surgery, slips from consciousness and enters heaven. When he awakes, he shares his experiences, to the amazement of his parents and others, who believe he's making up stories. Slowly, the child's father realizes the boy is telling the truth of what he's seen, including being seated in the lap of Jesus.

This film reflects my own childhood and adult wish, hope, or even belief: that once I die, I shall see again all those I love and have lost, and that I shall encounter the Christ. I realize I'm fantasizing, but it's remarkable that there are so many stories of those who've had near-death experiences and who recount similar experiences of seeing people they love and having a sense of peace and utter contentment.

I like to imagine that John is with me. I talk with him a great deal most days, especially when I experience something beautiful or encounter frustration or difficulty. There are times I hear his voice, laughing or saying, "Oh, sweetheart, don't let that get you down." And I'm comforted by that sense of his presence.

I've talked with others who have no belief in heaven but who nevertheless have experienced that "voice" of a lost loved one. NPR's legendary Susan Stamberg is one. She lost her beloved husband, Lou, to pancreatic cancer. He began complaining of stomach problems early in 2007, but after an initial exam he was told there were no indications of anything serious. Then in California the stomach discomfort recurred, and yet another medical check, but with the same diagnosis. When Susan and Lou returned home, the discomfort persisted. Finally, with examinations using what Susan called "the Big Machines," they were told Lou was suffering from pancreatic cancer, which, because the pancreas hides behind the stomach, is very hard to diagnose.

Lou underwent surgery in April 2007, but it was found that

the cancer had already metastasized, and that there was no effective chemotherapy. Nevertheless, he went through one round of chemo, then said he wanted no more. A very tough decision, but Susan said she knew it was the right one. The doctor advised her to take her husband home, since there was nothing more to be done.

Susan spoke of how difficult it was to watch the person she loved dying in front of her. At home, after about a week, he begged her to help him die, saying he had no desire to live through another hopeless day. But how could she help him? The two had spoken in earlier times about dying, each promising not to allow the other one to suffer and to help the other when the time came.

At this point, Susan said, she was frantic and irrational. Desperate to end his suffering. What could she do? "Here he was, begging me, and I felt helpless." Later, after Lou died, Susan realized that, because it was she who administered his morphine each day, she could have given him a larger dose than prescribed. She remembers clearly each dose she gave him and how careful she was to document it for the hospice nurse and doctor. Now she sees she could have given him extra morphine. She's still tormented by the question: Should she have done it? But she realizes that either she would have to live with the pain of not helping him or with the agony of watching him slowly die.

One night, at 3:00 a.m., Susan got out of bed to give Lou his last dose of morphine and then went back to sleep. When she awoke the next morning, Lou had died in his sleep. She had heard no sound, no crying out. Like me, she was not by her husband's side to hold his hand as he passed. But at least she is comforted by the thought that he died at home, in his own bed.

I told Susan what the nurses had told me when John died, that maybe those we love wait for us to be out of their presence before they die. She was in the next room. I was a mile or two away when John took his last breath.

"I wish I could hear his voice," Susan says. "I talk to much younger people about this, but talking to you who've gone through it feels comforting. We would have been married fifty-three years. A marriage goes through so many phases. Lou took early retirement, and when he did, our relationship changed. I'd never seen him as happy as he was during those twelve years of his retirement. He'd worked in government in the U.S. Agency for International Development. He was very tense and wound up much of the time. In retirement, he flourished. He bloomed. He joined various boards. He became involved with WAMU. He formed a French conversation group. His stress disappeared, which made us closer. We began to appreciate each other in new ways. Even our son, Josh, said he'd never seen his father so relaxed and happy."

Now that Susan's on her own, memories of that wonderful re-energized relationship have made his absence even harder for her.

Like Eleanor Clift, Susan said work was crucial to her. She went back after a month rather than "hanging around the house crying." She says she was "all over the place," and regards her first on-air report as sloppy. Slowly, seeing other people made the difference. She began to travel like crazy. She accepted any invitation she received. She just kept moving, and that helped.

On the other hand, coming into the Washington airport or returning to her home, she grieved all over again, because he wasn't there. "I do think I ran from grief. I wanted somehow to control it or put walls around it. When I stopped moving, it was all over me. I spent time in California with Josh. Lou and I used to go to Paris twice a year, and I was determined to go back, but it wasn't the same."

Coming home alone, she says, is the worst part. The Stamberg home is a cozy Sears, Roebuck house in Washington, D.C., in which she's lived for forty-three years. She never had much feeling for it, but now, she says, "it wraps itself around me."

I asked Susan her thoughts about heaven. She doesn't believe in "an afterlife where we all sit around and play cards." She says she wishes she *did* believe, and wishes she had a community and a rabbi to talk with.

I asked whether she actually talks with Lou, the way I talk with John. Rather, she says, she experiences Lou intervening when she's about to do something that could be damaging to her. She feels his presence and hears his voice—reminding her to sign the bottom of the check, or not to forget to turn off that light.

Recently, on my balcony, I saw a hummingbird for only the second time in my life. The first had been at the farm when John and I stood at the window overlooking the valley and saw a hummingbird together. I called my son to tell him about the hummingbird on the balcony, and his words were "Dad's spirit lives on!"

The other evening I was having dinner with a small group of women, all of whom were either widowed or divorced. The majority were younger than I. Marriage was the issue. Would any of them ever want to marry again? The answer: a clear and emphatic no. But to have another relationship was clearly a desire each of them had.

I had asked Susan Stamberg whether she'd ever want to date. "Lou's been gone seven years now. I have a million women friends, but I miss the male presence. I actually joined JDate. It was disastrous!" After an article about her appeared in the *Washington Post*, a friend told her she would get tons of reaction because she had said she was lonely. There was just one letter to which she responded, a letter that began, "I can't believe I'm doing this. . . ." She met the gentleman for coffee, and their relationship has become very satisfying. Susan spoke about feeling "ready" now.

She met another man through friends, and began having feelings for him. He was "kind of closed off," and not conversant with things she loved, but he was there. He was tall and he was steady and reliable. Though the relationship ended, Susan says, "I'm grateful to him because he made me feel alive." But the way it ended, she says, "might make me more wary next time." One more thing: she misses the intimacy of sex, being that close to someone.

Finally, she says, it's important for her to have a place to go, to work or volunteer, to see people. "It was all lonely in the beginning, with and without people. Something was missing. I'd become the focus of attention wherever I went, but I wasn't the most important person in anybody's life anymore. When I go out for a walk, there's no longer anybody in the world who knows where I am. I miss the mirror that Lou was."

And what about the house? I ask. Do you want to keep it? "Josh wants me to sell it, and before he died, Lou said to get out of the house. Move to a condo. Since he died, I've looked a lot, and still look from time to time. There's so much that's nice in California, where Josh lives. But I have my network here. I have a few friends out there, but here I have a history, and nothing like that in California. It makes all the difference. My son has two children. He's an actor. His schedule is crazy. I don't want to bother him."

As for me, I really can't imagine myself having any other intimate relationship. Relationships take work, and, at this point in my life, I have enough to do just taking care of myself. But as they always say, never say never!

~ A Cutting Board

My Darling Scoop,

Last night I reached for a board on which to chop some vegetables. The usual small board was wet, so I pulled out another from the cupboard, one I hadn't laid eyes on in many months. It was the board you used for years and years to cut the bottoms off asparagus. There was a deep indentation in it, at exactly the point you used to mark how long the asparagus should be. That board must be at least fifty years old. I know we had it when we moved from our tiny house on Saratoga Avenue to our home on Worthington Drive.

How can a simple wooden board contain so many memories? Not only did you use it for cutting asparagus but, on the many weekends we cooked together, that board was always the first to come out. Whether we were making lentil soup (your favorite for at least five years), chicken stew, or veal-shank stew, chopping carrots, making ratatouille, or slicing celery, that board was always on the counter, by your side.

How precious were our moments of cooking together, listening to classical music, watching a football game, listening to the news on NPR, sometimes talking, sometimes not. You taught me to cook, my love. I came to the marriage making, according to you, "the best scrambled eggs" you'd ever tasted. Other than that, my skills were thin, to be kind about it.

From the start of our relationship we began shopping

together, selecting foods (some, like veal kidneys, oysters, clams, I'd never tasted in my life), and then cooking them together. I began as the sous chef, doing most of the preparation leading up to the actual cooking. But slowly our roles began to reverse, and I took over the major part of the cooking itself.

We experimented with a variety of foods. I remember one particular disaster we had when we were first married, living in your aunt's home on R Street NW. You were determined to prepare tripe (defined by Oxford as "the first or second stomach of a ruminant, especially a cow"). I'm game, I thought, and off we went to the French Market on Wisconsin Avenue. You began cooking the tripe and I began smelling it. In fact, the smell overwhelmed the entire house, an absolutely awful, almost putrid, smell. You finally conceded that something had gone wrong in the preparation, and you disposed of the sad remains.

By contrast, we learned to make so many good dishes together, and always with such careful preparation. Tomatoes stuffed with spinach and pine nuts, blanquette de veau, English trifle. I remember how, for parties, I'd always leave the decoration of the food platters to you, whether it was Easter, Christmas, or an anniversary. And people raved. You were so artistic, and I depended on you for your brilliant eye. I think Jennie got her artistic ability from you, while David inherited your methodical approach to problem solving.

It's the times when we were cooking together—and working in the garden—that I remember most vividly. They were two activities we both loved and enjoyed helping each other with. Whether it was digging a hole in which to insert a new azalea, seasoning a stew, testing out the sweetness of my Christmas baklava, you always made sure things were just the way they should be.

It was so distressing that one of the effects of your Parkinson's disease was that your taste buds went dull. Parkinson's also took away your sense of smell, so you could no longer enjoy the wonderful aroma of my sour-cream coffee cake baking in the oven.

Toward the end of your time here at the apartment, your back began to hurt so badly that you could no longer stand long enough to cut, chop, or slice vegetables, so you would sit in the kitchen with me as I did the chopping and slicing. As time went on, your food choices narrowed, and with that narrowing we lost another aspect of the joy we'd experienced early in our married life.

Now, my darling Scoop, food without you beside me to enjoy it with is not the same experience. I eat because I must, and I dine on foods that are easy to prepare or, indeed, already prepared. I miss sharing meals with you. I miss watching you take a bite of something and smile your approval. I miss the memories of preparing food with you. I miss your stopping to hug and kiss me in the middle of food preparation, to put your hands gently on my breasts and caress them. Food meant so much to both of us, back then.

∾ New Friendships

*L*ast night, for the first time since John died, I invited a few friends in my building for dinner. For the past couple of years, several of us have gotten together periodically to share dinner in each of our apartments. Since it's late August, near the end of summer, I told them I'd be serving my favorite easy supper: Popeyes spicy fried chicken. We all love throwing away our diets for playtime, and that's what this was.

One friend made divine deviled eggs, another brought tomatoes, basil, and mozzarella on skewers, and a third contributed a delicious chocolate ice cream. Also on the menu: black bean salad and hot-spicy coleslaw. It was a feast we enjoyed out on my balcony. The weather, though it had rained during the day, was clear and comfortable.

How important these new friendships have become in my life. I'm so thankful to have connected with so many people here in my condo after moving here in 2008. How does one find new friends in a condo after living in one neighborhood for forty years? Sometimes it happens accidentally. In my case, I was talking to Bridgit Fitzgerald, a woman I knew who was working at Neiman Marcus, and happened to mention to her that we were looking at condominiums, and especially liked the one where she herself lived.

She promised to be on the lookout for me, and indeed she kept that promise, calling me urgently one evening to tell me that the apartment we eventually purchased was about to come on the market.

That first connection helped connect me to other people in the building, a number of whom have become social acquaintances and some good friends, though forming new relationships at my age is no easy task. Some of these people are younger than I am, and have already retired. I served on our board of directors, and through that activity became involved in the life of the building and its residents.

I know myself to be an outgoing person at heart. At the same time, however, John's death has created a greater need for quiet time, away from all friends, activities, and involvements. I am increasingly seeking solitude, something I would never have imagined myself doing or enjoying. When I was writing my first book, *Finding My Voice,* I remember feeling a sense of dread when I was surrounded by quiet. Now, on Saturdays and Sundays, I recall John's saying that, for him, silence was like a drink of water. I'm feeling that same sense of wholeness these times when I can think and reflect for hours, without talking to a single soul.

The balance between involvement, activity, and time for myself is what I'm learning to capture. It's in that balance that I think I can bring some harmony into my life. For so long I've been rushing—to do everything, to be everywhere, to join everyone. Now I've become far more selective, desiring to spend more time in the quiet of my apartment, while still spending enough time with friends to maintain the relationships.

To my mind, there's an apt comparison to the consumption of food. I think I'm moving to greater sensitivity in finding what satisfies my appetite rather than my cravings. I know I tend to consume more food when I'm with others—perhaps being in company enhances the appetite. But I also know I'm happier when I consume less. My whole body feels content with less.

In the months before his death, John was eating almost nothing. He had no appetite even for his beloved salmon but chose to combine various vegetables, followed always by a big dish of ice cream. We laughed together about his being the only person we knew who could eat ice cream twice a day and *still* lose weight.

As for friendships, John had very few, and that kept our circle of friends relatively small. Once Parkinson's disease set in, he manifested an even greater reserve when I would introduce him to new friends I'd made or persuade him to go out to dinner with people just outside our inner group. It was as though he couldn't afford to allow people access to him, as if he would have to expend too much energy to be receptive to an unknown entity. My good fortune has been to be able to rely on old and dear friends like the Busbys, while making new friends like Trish and George Vradenburg.

The Vradenburgs are cofounders of USAgainstAlzheimer's, a nonprofit organization they're funding on their own to help wipe out the dreaded disease that is striking so many of us. Our meeting was totally serendipitous. The three of us, George, Trish, and I, had been invited to participate in a fashion show at Brooks Brothers on Connecticut Avenue in Washington, to benefit the campaign against Alzheimer's.

Each of us spoke casually, exchanging names, humorous words about what we were doing, but nothing very personal.

When the show was over, I was about to leave the store when George followed me out to say that they would very much like to have my e-mail address. I readily gave it to him, and several days later Trish contacted me, and we had the first of a series of lunches together, forming an immediate deep bond of friendship.

As our friendship began to blossom, Trish, a former scriptwriter for *Designing Women* and other television sitcoms, told me she'd written a play about her mother's descent into Alzheimer's. The play, called *Surviving Grace,* had been performed off-Broadway in New York, and now she wanted to stage a reading of it at the Phillips Collection in Washington as a fund-raiser for the organization she and her husband had established. She asked whether I might take a look at it and give her my thoughts. And so I did.

I thought it was a wonderful play, mostly telling the heart-wrenching story of her mother's slide from being a politically and socially active woman in New York and Washington to being one whose descent into Alzheimer's prompted her then husband (Trish's father) to have her institutionalized, divorce her, and marry a much younger woman. It was a heartbreaking story.

After I read the play and told Trish how much I loved it, I suggested a few changes that I felt would make it more adaptable to a Washington audience. We spent several afternoons going over it word by word, phrase by phrase, which was a brand-new experience for me. I enjoyed every minute of it. After we'd finished, I was astounded when Trish asked me if I would take the part of the mother for the reading at the Phillips. I was thrilled to be asked, and thrilled to accept.

Around that same time, the actress Marilu Henner, who had appeared in several television productions, including *Taxi,* published a book about her phenomenal gift of memory. After she came on my program, I wondered whether she might agree to appear in the play. She did, and we were on our way. Our reading of the first act of *Surviving Grace* raised $150,000 for USAgainstAlzheimer's, and since then we've read the play to audiences in Los Angeles and San Diego, in Raleigh and Indianapolis and then Boston.

This is really a dream come true for me. Several years ago, a large coffee-table book of photographs was published consisting of prominent women each stating her most-fantasized achievement. I was one of those women, and I was dressed in a long gown, holding a fake Oscar. Who knows? Who says dreams can't come true?

However unlikely an Oscar, this new experience has fed my soul. Appearing onstage, reading this extraordinarily moving and funny play, has allowed me to think in new ways about the future and its possibilities. The folds of my life are still opening.

⤳ Healing

Speaking with those who have lost a spouse or partner or someone else to whom they were very close seems inevitably to come around to the same question: How have you managed to heal? In several instances, the answers were similar to my own approach: work, travel, reach out to old and new friends. Steady activity seemed to be the response I got most often.

Susan Stamberg wrote: "It really is *work* that has been most healing. Work, and a tremendous amount of travel in the first year or two after Lou died. Steady activity is what I was after. I felt if I stopped, I'd be overwhelmed by grief. I wish I had a wiser answer, but I don't. Friends, family, work. That's it."

But what about those who aren't working—who may have retired or, indeed, have *never* worked outside the home?

For Roger Mudd, who retired from his radio and television work several years ago, the answer was a reflective one: "Our life together was so rich, so deep, so respectful of each other that I would be letting E.J. down if I didn't carry on as before with our family and our friends who so admired her. What I found totally surprising was how I learned from her friends, through their stories and reminiscences, qualities and strengths that were quite different from what I remember. That made her all the more alive to me." Roger does indeed "carry on."

Several months after E.J.'s death, Roger invited a number of close friends to dinner, setting the table with all the beautiful crystal and china that she had always so elegantly displayed. We toasted her, talked of her, looked around the beautiful room, and felt her presence.

I, too, have found that entertaining friends can be part of the healing process. For months prior to his move to Brighton Gardens, John expressed reluctance at our holding dinner parties or cocktail gatherings, primarily because he no longer felt he had much to offer. He would barely converse, quite often leaving the room to return to bed. In deference, then, I invited only a very few close friends to be with us.

After he died, I realized how much I'd missed the joy of having people here in the apartment. I'm sure it goes back to my Arab upbringing, the many occasions when my dad's brothers and sisters came to our home and were always entertained so warmly by my mother. Whether it's just a few close friends for an easy supper on the balcony in good weather or a more formal gathering in the dining room with as many as twelve people at the table, or a large buffet gathering of forty, I love to entertain, and that has helped me get through my periods of loneliness following John's death.

First and foremost, however, I know that work has been my survival mechanism, the crucial part of my healing process. I realize how fortunate I am at my age to be able to go on working at something I love, with people I admire, producing a program that reaches millions around the world.

I do admit that getting up each morning at 5:00 is difficult—it takes a solid ten minutes before I can feel good about the coming day. During those moments I question why I keep on "keeping on," relishing the fantasy of forgetting it all and going back to sleep. But I know how important it is to continue being involved with the world through my work. And when I am no longer employed as a broadcaster, I believe I will find other activities to keep me occupied.

I will definitely want to contribute in some ways to Compassion & Choices, a national organization working to give people the right to choose to die with medical assistance. I so strongly believe in our right to choose when we die, if our illness is beyond any hope of bringing back a fullness of health. I know and respect those who argue that suffering is a part of living, but I do not agree and will do my best to speak out. I myself don't want to suffer, nor do I want my family to see me suffer. When I believe the time has come for me to say farewell to this beautiful world, I will do so.

Alzheimer's and Parkinson's are two of the most terrible diseases marking this world, and against which I want to continue to work. I intend to do all I can to speak on behalf of patients who have been stricken with these physical and mind-depleting disorders, and to participate in the ongoing search for new treatments beyond the virtually nonexistent ones we have now.

Years ago I began learning to draw and to paint with watercolors. Someday I'll return to that. I love handicrafts. I've embroidered a number of pieces that are here in the apartment. I'd like to learn to quilt. And I'd like to learn more about flower arranging.

I recognize that I have choices. Not everyone who is left a widow or widower has the opportunities I have, or the good health to go on looking for new avenues of expression. And for me, finding ways to stay involved with people has been key throughout my lifetime, not just recently. I've had to learn to be alone long before now, doing more for and *by* myself than I ever imagined doing. And I know that my sense of independence and my strength, for now at least, depend on my ability to continue to function in my various roles and with all of my responsibilities, free of reliance on others.

⤳ Grief Counseling

W hen John died, I didn't seek assistance from counselors. I had talked so much and so often with friends and our children during his illness that I believe I had been grieving for years—grieving for the loss of the man I knew. Grieving for his spirit, his vitality, his energy, his laughter. By the time he moved to Brighton Gardens, most of that spirit had left him.

My grieving came in the form of tightness—in my throat, in my every muscle. I could barely move my neck. I had headaches every day. I could sense the lack of freedom within me, the rigid feeling of having too much to do, too many decisions to make, and not enough time to think about what was going to happen. Months before John died, our son asked me, "So how will you be when Dad dies?" I'll be okay, I said, knowing that I wouldn't allow myself at that time to fully consider what or how I might be. I just knew I had to be strong. I couldn't fall apart. I have too many responsibilities, both professional and personal. I have an apartment to care for. I have a tiny dog who depends on my love. I have grandchildren who enjoy my company. And, not least of all, there are all those people who, every day, turn on their radios to hear my voice.

Six months after John died I attended a grief counseling group. I wanted to listen, to learn whether such a group could help me in ways I couldn't imagine.

On the evening I attended there were four participants, including myself, plus the counselor. We sat together in a small, warmly lit room, with only the occasional sounds of outside laughter drifting into our otherwise quiet surroundings. We introduced ourselves. One other woman was new to the group. She began by talking about the many losses she'd experienced over the past few years, how paralyzed she felt, at times wanting just to stay in her bed, under blankets and pillows, waiting for the days to pass. Another woman spoke of having recently received her late husband's ashes, which she intended to take back to his home state the following week. He had died swiftly, from pancreatic cancer. The third talked of losing her mother, and the grief she went on feeling over the end of a relationship that had never been fully realized. Now, with only a sister to share her memories, she wanted to come closer to her mother, but wasn't sure whether this was possible.

When my turn came to speak, I talked of the long illness John had endured, how Parkinson's had weakened him physically, but how he had continued to enjoy life up until the last few months, when his spirits began to sag. I spoke briefly about our marriage, the imperfections that we, like all couples, experienced, and then I spoke of his dying days, the most difficult ones I've ever lived through.

Watching John in those last few days of his life, after he'd decided he would no longer eat or drink, after he'd lapsed into sleep, I confessed, had made me angry. Why hadn't he been able to be "put to sleep"? Why did our laws infringe upon an individual's choice to die when dying is inevitable, as it was in his case, within a few months?

The more I talked, the more I realized just how angry I really am about his not having been allowed to go in a more dignified manner. And there, in that group, I felt safe declaring my anger. I was not being judged or argued with or presented with someone else's point of view. I could simply express my strong feelings for the right to die as one wishes without having some politician or medical doctor talk to me about the "slippery slope" or putting people to death.

This, it seems to me, is the greatest reward of attending a grief counseling group: knowing that you won't be judged. We're all so different in the ways we express our humanity, and we manifest those differences in the ways we express our grief. Some may sob, while others may sit stoically. Through my losses over the years I've learned to allow myself to feel the grief and, to a certain extent, share it with those I'm close to. But I've never wanted to fully express my sadness to others, even when my mother and father died so close to each other. Indeed, one dear friend chastised me for not allowing myself to open up and talk about the loneliness I find myself feeling.

Instead, I cry when I'm alone. I talk with John about my sadness as though he were here. I tell him how much I miss him. I remind him—and myself—of the many wonderful experiences we enjoyed together, even through the tough times. I look at photographs, I sing songs we loved, I watch movies again that we watched together. All to be with him, to stay within arm's reach, to believe he's still here with me.

For each of the others in the counseling group, there was an apparent need for outward expression of grief, but I didn't feel that need. Perhaps it was because John had been ill for so long that when he died I was relieved, both for him and for myself. That's an awful thing to say about myself, but it's true. I was relieved. I would no longer have to watch his daily decline, see him struggle to keep food in his mouth, ache for him as he tried to move from bed to bathroom. His struggles became so acute that when he finally decided he wanted it over, I totally understood and supported his decision.

Had the group been one I'd been part of for a long time, I believe I might have reacted differently and allowed myself to open up my deepest feelings. As it was, I couldn't really share myself completely. At the end of the hour and a half, the group counselor led us in a five-minute silent meditation, breathing deeply, trying to allow ourselves to shake off negative feelings, to go back into the world with some peace of mind. Asked if I would be returning to the group the following week, I said I wasn't sure. But I knew I wouldn't. Certainly not because I didn't like the people, but because I wanted to keep my thoughts and feelings inside myself.

I don't want to lose any of John, I don't want to "get over" my deep sense of loss. Instead, I want to incorporate it into my everyday behavior. And I believe that living through the loss is helping me to become a stronger and more compassionate person, more self-reliant, less dependent on others. And helping me to take charge of my own feelings, to learn to live with them.

As I left the building, I was happy to breathe in the cool night air. And happy to be alone.

∾ *What's Next?*

I wonder whether all those who lose a partner are asked questions about the future, such as Will you sell your home? Will you move to be near your children? Will you retire? I'm sure they all are, and I'm no exception, either in doing the asking or in being asked. This much I know: I'll make no changes for at least a year. Over and over I've heard professionals make that recommendation, and it makes total sense to me. Even now, I'm not sufficiently in touch with my feelings to know what will be right for me in the coming years. For the moment, I know that I'll want to keep my life moving along at a moderate-to-rapid pace. That's what keeps sadness at bay.

So I continue to enjoy the life I lead, one that is rich both professionally and personally. I go to the studio each day with gratitude and anticipation, looking forward to seeing and meeting with my co-workers, running over in my own mind the coming interviews and the latest news that might affect what I do on the air. All of that forces me to go on being aware of what's happening in the world, and that in and of itself is life-enhancing, because it keeps me in the present, not dwelling on the past.

Once those two hours on the air are over, there are office tasks to complete and errands to run, just to keep daily life going smoothly. None of us really likes change, and I'm certainly happy in my daily routine. However, at some point this will change. I know the time is coming when I will step back from the daily broadcast, leaving my on-air responsibilities to someone with fresh ideas and new approaches. I'm not thinking of complete retirement, but am starting to imagine what my life will be like when *The Diane Rehm Show* is no more.

Many of us face this challenge at some point in our lives: how to rearrange a life that's been professionally focused for so many years to one that allows us more time to choose how and where to focus our energies. It's a time I'm beginning to plan for. One difficulty is that I've never planned any aspect of my life—it's all just happened! So the idea that now I must begin to look ahead feels somewhat out of character. One part of me believes the next chapter will take care of itself, though talking seriously with financial planners can quickly divest one of that feeling.

Even so, I do believe that something new will arrive that will involve my abilities, whatever they are and however they are seen by others. Something new and engrossing.

Why this optimism on my part? I think, in part, it's because John instilled it in me. At some of the worst moments in my career in broadcasting, when it nearly all came crashing down because of the chronic voice problems I began suffering in 1998, or the frustration became more than I felt I could bear, John would always reassure me that there would be better days ahead.

That was, of course, when I was a younger woman. Now the question becomes how many more opportunities will be available to me as the beginning of my ninth decade draws near. I may be healthy and energetic now, but who can know what the future may bring? That, for me, is both the challenge and the excitement.

Many people have asked me when I intend to retire. Now, at age seventy-eight, I can say I'm addressing the question.

I can continue to host a daily two-hour NPR program until the end of 2016, when my contract expires, and I definitely plan to carry on through the next elections, and then find some other means by which I can make a contribution to society. I will take my days one at a time, dwelling in the richness of the work experience I still enjoy. One thing I *am* certain of is that when I do finally retire from my daily radio work, I will find other interesting activities to keep me busy.

I'm reading the work of Ellen Langer, a brilliant and courageous Harvard psychologist, known as the Mother of Mindfulness. One of the many experiments she's performed involved having eight men in their seventies live in a completely closed-off environment, as if they were twenty-two again. Bruce Grierson wrote about this experiment in the *New York Times Magazine*'s Health Issue late in 2014. The men lived for five days in a converted monastery in New Hampshire, surrounded by the music and the black-and-white television of the late fifties. Each man was physically and emotionally evaluated before and after the five days. They were encouraged to "be" the persons they had been years earlier. For the most part, they came away not only feeling younger but *looking* younger, sitting up straighter, walking taller, and actually seeing better.

I take from this experiment what I think has been the saving grace of my work, my ongoing activities, my engagement with friends: I have remained involved. I go on getting out of bed very early every morning, I have a shower, eat my breakfast, get dressed, and then *put on my makeup*! Of course there are weekend days when I don't have to bother with "dressing up" or putting on makeup, and, to be honest, on those days I rejoice. But I also know that I really don't feel as perky on the weekends as I do on workdays. How I look, I realize, is how I feel!

There are many widows and single women living in my building. Many of them are beautifully dressed, made up, and coiffed each and every day. Others take less care of how they look. What makes the strongest impression on me is realizing that those women, whether younger or older, who *do* take care of their looks seem more outgoing, more pleasant, even happier. Is it because they *look* better? Or do they dress and use makeup because they *feel* better when they do?

Putting on makeup, shaping my eyes, using mascara and lipstick, all make me look better—that I know for certain.

I also know that wearing high heels is part of what makes me feel good about myself. My friends think I'm crazy, and are forever saying things like "How can you stand to wear those high-heeled shoes?" Well, I've been wearing them since I was sixteen. I love high heels, perhaps in the same way my mother, who was much shorter than I am, loved wearing them. I walk well in them, I walk taller, and, more important, they make me feel good. Maybe taking the time and the effort to *look* better helps me to *feel* younger, stronger, more spirited. Whatever it is that's propelling me to take the time to dress carefully, wear appropriate makeup, and fix my hair, I will keep on doing it.

The other day I heard the writer Isabel Allende give a TED Talk on NPR. Afterward she spoke with the host, Guy Raz, about her attitudes toward aging. She spoke about saying yes to whatever comes her way, including love or even loss of life. In

1994, she wrote a memoir about the loss of her beloved daughter, Paula, who fell into a coma from the disease porphyria and never recovered.

I was so moved by her comments regarding women, who she said "become invisible as we get older." We must, she said, "accept life and make the best of it." She spoke of how the mind lives on even as the body ages. Our lives are infected with "the fear of suffering," but in that fear we "lose out on the joy as well." She talked of how she enjoys the body she has at this moment, at age seventy-one, and refuses to think of herself as frail. "Death is in the neighborhood, or even in my house," she said, but in retirement, she argues, it's passion that keeps one alive.

Engagement and working with an open heart, wisdom, and spirit from Isabel Allende. Just what I needed to hear.

❧ Losing a Friend

S hortly after John moved to Brighton Gardens in early November 2012, I lost Jane Dixon, my dearest friend in the world. She died in her sleep on Christmas morning. Jane and I had been the closest of friends for forty-five years. We met at St. Patrick's Episcopal Church, where we both became very involved not only because of our children but because there was an active social life built around the church community.

Almost from the day we met, we began sharing our stories with each other, she from Winona, Mississippi, where her father was the town doctor. Jane grew up knowing she was adored and cared for. She got an outstanding education at Randolph-Macon College and Vanderbilt University, then married a southern boy, David Dixon. But she yearned to break free from the segregated South, and so they moved to Washington, D.C.

We were two young homemakers in the 1960s, both feeling the frustrated need to do "something more." We talked on the phone practically each day, pouring out what seemed unattainable dreams we had for our futures, realizing that, eventually, our children would be on their own.

Shortly after I began my volunteer work at WAMU, Jane declared her goal: to become an Episcopal priest. Not only did she accomplish that after years of intense study at Virginia Theological Seminary, but years later she was consecrated as only the second female bishop of the Episcopal Church. Her

inner beauty was palpable, and her loving-kindness and generous heart radiated to all of us who knew and loved her.

On December 25, 2012, my phone rang at 8:00 a.m. Looking
at my caller ID, I assumed it was Jane herself calling to wish me
a Merry Christmas, so I answered with a very cheery hello, and
was surprised to hear not Jane's voice but that of her daughter,
Mary Dixon Raibman.

I'll never forget her words. "Ms. Rehm, I have some very,
very sad news. My mommy died in her sleep this morning." To
say I was stunned simply cannot express what I felt when I heard
those words. I just could not believe my darling friend was gone.
Mary went on to say that they'd had an all-family celebration the
night before, and that Jane had gone to bed at 9:30 p.m., saying
she felt "very, very tired."

And that was it. She never woke up.

No one will ever be sure what happened to her, whether a
blood clot had traveled to her brain or whether her heart just
gave out. She was gone.

I can hardly think of that day without weeping. Jane and I
were not just the most intimate of friends; we loved each other
as though we were sisters. In fact, we had often said that each
of us was the sister the other had never had, the one who was
always there for the other. Through hardship and illness and loss
we'd stood right there beside each other.

Her laughter was infectious. We celebrated so many birth-
days and holidays together, always bursting into laughter at the
slightest reference to a memory we shared. She was a mag-
nificent storyteller, which helped make her sermons so powerful. She loved clothes as much as I do, and we loved cooking

together, as we had done for church suppers in the early days of
our friendship.

Her memorial service filled Washington National Cathedral.
So many had been touched by her warmth and love! They lined
up by the hundreds to honor her and her memory.

As for me, the loss was devastating. We'd always joked that,
when we got older, we'd all live together under one roof, hire
people to help us with our daily lives, and sit back and enjoy
telling each other stories. And up to a point, that is exactly what
happened.

We ended up living in the same condominium, so that whenever either of us felt the need for a chat, we'd meet in the lobby
or sit outside in the beautiful park that is part of our condo
grounds. We could enjoy each other's company, and I could
share the concerns that were growing in my mind regarding
John's physical and emotional health.

To say that I felt bereft when Jane died is an understate-
ment. I felt abandoned—doubly lost, because she'd been such
a support when John moved into assisted living. She helped me
through the emotional transition by going with me to see him,
by offering him Holy Communion, by talking frankly and honestly with us about how our lives were changing.

In her gentle, pastoral way, she could reach John, who was,
after all, her godson. With Jane I could weep openly. She was
there to help me shed the shell I had armored myself with, just
to keep life on track. The shock of her death, coming as it did on
Christmas Day, with no warning, was utterly wrenching. I felt as
though my own heart was bleeding.

It was partly due to these feelings that I began to wonder

whether those who lose a loved one suddenly grieve in different ways from those who watch a loved one go gradually. I know from talks with her husband how hard it was for him to lose her as he did. Now Dixie has been forced to rethink his very existence without Jane. He tells me how awful it is to walk into their apartment and not hear her voice calling out to him, instead only silence.

I, by contrast, had a year and a half to learn to live alone, and during that period I knew I could pick up the phone and speak to John, or leave work and drive over to Brighton Gardens to see him. I had months to observe his decline, to watch his painful efforts to move, to walk, to eat. Occasionally he would agree to be wheeled outdoors to the garden, where we could sit together to listen to the waterfall, to be with Maxie, to remark on the beautiful spring weather. We had time to talk openly and honestly about our marriage, what we'd done right, what we'd done wrong, and how much time we'd wasted being incapable of finding peace with each other. Did that span of time and those precious moments together make John's death easier on me? Perhaps.

For Dixie, whose marriage to Jane was very different from John's and mine, the fact that death came so suddenly, with Jane in apparent good health, and immediately after a wonderful family gathering, was an enormous shock, not just to the heart but to an entire way of life. Who can say that he would have grieved less for her had she suffered a long illness, as John did?

As we grew older, Jane and I had talked about how our lives might end. She knew that John's mother had taken her own life, and I said that, should I face an untreatable illness, I would do the same. She expressed doubt that she would have the courage to end her own life. But one thing was certain: she did not want to grow so old that she would have to move into a nursing home and be taken care of. She actually dreaded the idea of growing old.

John was my partner, my spouse, my beloved husband, with whom I'd gone through many struggles to maintain our marriage. Jane was my dear friend, my sister, on whom I relied for strength and sustenance. John died slowly. Jane's death was instantaneous. Who can say which death was harder to grapple with? I know only that I've lost them both.

*T*oday is John's birthday. He would have been eighty-four years old. A former law partner of his, Will Leonard, sent me this e-mail: "I shall always remember the date, because it is the birth date of two of the most remarkable men I have ever known; two of whom I tried, but failed miserably, to emulate. One was my father. The other was your great husband. My best wishes to you on what undoubtedly will be a day of sad, and, hopefully, happy, remembrances."

And that is precisely what it was. When I woke this morning, my first thought was, Today is John's birthday. I wished him a happy birthday, out loud. Maxie, lying on the bed with me, took that as an indication that on this early Sunday morning I was finally ready to get up. He came and kissed me on the cheek, his funny furry face and lovable doggy smell pressing me to rise. Part of me longed to stay put under the covers, shutting out reality and allowing me to go on talking with John. In the days before Parkinson's, we had many of our sweetest conversations in our bed, early in the morning on weekends, when neither of us had to rush to get up. I was imagining how many questions I would ask now, if he could hear me.

How are you? Has the journey been what you'd hoped it might be? Is that new world as peaceful and as filled with light as we here on earth want to imagine? Can you "feel"? Are you strong? Does it matter? Can you see me? Can you understand how I have been longing to speak with you? Do you know I keep your pictures on the piano, and speak to you every time I pass them?

The fact is that most people who've lost family members struggle when encountering the first birthday or important holiday after a death. For me, John's birthday compounds my sadness of the season. My mother died on January 1, 1956, at age forty-nine. My father died eleven months later, at age sixty-two, literally of a broken heart. Now, as I experience my first Thanksgiving after John's death, I feel as though gravel is churning in the pit of my stomach, preparing to unleash or heave back all the stored memories of holidays, happy and otherwise. How do we deal with the absence of a loved one on a day when that absence is so deeply felt? I remembered each step of the day.

At 5:00 on Thanksgiving morning, John would arise to take the turkey from the refrigerator, making sure it would be ready when I came to the kitchen to stuff it and get it ready for roasting. We would together have chopped the celery, mushrooms, and onions the day before, and now I would lightly sauté them in butter. I would cook the gizzards for an hour, saving some of the liquid to moisten the vegetables and bread crumbs.

Then came John's important moment: tasting for seasoning, which consisted of sage, poultry seasoning, salt, and pepper. The dressing had to be slightly oversalted to account for loss of seasoning during the roasting process. The butter melted and the basting began, every half hour. The day before Thanksgiving, I prepared Craig Claiborne's recipe for cranberry-orange relish, as well as Jane Dixon's mother-in-law's baked squash recipe (Jane said it was the only good thing her mother-in-law ever gave her), ready to bake the next day. As the turkey roasted, the apples for pies were peeled, cored, and sliced, a task that John, David, and Jennie all performed, while I made the pastry. Into the smaller oven went the pies, timed so they'd still be warm when we finished our turkey.

Of course, I'm reaching back in time, reaching back to before John grew weak, when he was still able to lift the twenty-five-pound bird from the oven. In fact, many of my memories of him have begun to shift from *after* he became ill to *before*. I *want* to remember him as he was when he was younger and stronger, not necessarily in his twenties or thirties but in his forties and fifties, before any back problems or operations, before any slowing down or shuffling.

I want to remember him as he swung a pickax to break up the driveway in front of our house on Worthington Drive. I want to see him as he hauled a wheelbarrow full of tree trimmings at the farm or when he lifted large pieces of rock to repair the stone wall. I want to feel his arms as he carried me up the stairs at our first dwelling in Georgetown. I want to hear again that loud voice that had offended me when we first met.

But the holidays, beginning in early November, instead bring on such sadness. For years, I would get ill every Christmas. One of our therapists used to say, "The body remembers." My sadness was always so great around that time of year, as I remembered my mother's and father's deaths, that I would find myself plummeting down and further down into dark thoughts, dark feelings, and, eventually, illness. Even after I became aware, through therapy, of this pattern, the illnesses went on occurring.

I can remember one Christmas Eve when I was so sick I couldn't join John, David, and Jennie for midnight services.

Perhaps those illnesses were the only way I could deal with the unspoken grief I went on feeling, even after all those years— feelings of loss so great that I felt like an orphan, someone with nobody to care for me. And my body would collapse.

So now I must add another loss, of the one with whom I've lived for most of my life. This year I spent Thanksgiving Day with dear friends. When it came time to say grace, our host included the names of those who had died in the past year, including the name of John Rehm. Instantly, I saw John carving the turkey in the kitchen, using *his* father's knife, with David watching, learning. Moments like those, happy, anticipatory moments—those are the ones I choose to remember.

∽ The Christmas Holidays

*E*ven before the most celebratory holiday of the year arrives, I'm forced to confront our wedding anniversary, December 19, and memories of that frigid day when we were married in 1959. I find myself recalling every detail, not only what each of us wore and the food we ate, but the beauty of the day, so sunny and crisp, the behavior of every guest, the reflections in the mirrors of the elegant dining room where we had our wedding dinner.

We had vowed not to see or speak with each other that day until the moment of the ceremony, so it was John's mother who called to ask whether I wanted him to wear his vest with his brand-new suit. Of course, I said, do have him wear his vest. The Reverend Duncan Howlett, who was extremely active in the civil rights movement, married us at All Souls Unitarian Church in Washington, in a service attended by some thirty guests. The photographer never showed up, so all our memories of that day remained our own internal real or imagined snapshots and recollections, which we loved to go over in detail each year.

But of all the events hard to endure in the months following John's death, nothing could be worse than Christmas. On the day after Thanksgiving, as I worked around the apartment, I turned on the radio and heard my first Christmas carol. I burst into tears. Now it really hits. Hard. Christmas without John. Singing carols together in the kitchen. Hearing the wonderful songs, again and again, never tiring of them. Remembering all the Christmas Eves at St. Patrick's Episcopal Church, with the children at our side.

Every evening I lie on the floor at the foot of my bed doing exercises to strengthen my back. Tonight I listen to the Brahms Violin Concerto, the very recording (on vinyl) that John gave me the first Christmas of our budding relationship. He'd left Washington to be with his parents in Pennsylvania at his father's farm. I was alone, and chose to be alone, in the tiny apartment I briefly lived in after my first husband and I had separated.

On that Christmas Day of 1958, despite invitations from cousins and friends to be with them, I had decided to stay alone, to experience the emptiness around me. I can remember sitting in my living room, listening to this concerto again and again, responding to its extraordinary beauty and complexity. I had never heard it before, but on this day, I felt its depth and its lush intensity reaching into me.

Now, lying on the floor on this evening in early December 2014, contemplating my first Christmas without John, listening to this gorgeous rendition once again, I hear it with a new sense of loss. Not as a young woman falling in love, but as a woman approaching her eighties, feeling the intensity of grieving for a lover, a husband, a partner. I wish he were here to listen to this music with me, though we wouldn't utter a word to each other; we would just sit and listen, and then he would remind me—or I him—that this was the first real gift he ever gave to me.

I hope that someday I can learn to be "in the moment," as so many have described it, as John could be when he listened to music. I remember the very first concert he invited me to, at the

Library of Congress, where I watched him listening so intensely. I sat astounded, just glancing at him, realizing how caught up he was in that music, those sounds, that performance. I've rarely had that feeling, but tonight it has come over me, taking me into an almost rapturous state.

All my friends have been extremely solicitous, repeating to me what I already know and now hear again and again: the first year of holidays, with all the memories of rituals, church services, decorations, and, most especially, music, is very difficult.

My heart goes back in time to when Jennie was just six years old, when we began creating our own Christmas cards. That was the year she did her very first drawing for us, a wonderfully zany snowman, a reindeer, an extremely contemporary rendition of a pine tree, and a star. The four of us took colored pens and added zest to each of the figures, on all two hundred cards.

That began a tradition that continues to this day. Jennie's daughter, Sarah, my thirteen-year-old granddaughter, has created a charming card for 2014, which in some ways reminds me of the very first one. Until I saw it I wasn't even sure I wanted to send out cards this year. Normally I would write a letter to go along with the card, to bring all our friends up-to-date on what's happened during the year with the Rehm family. But don't they already *know*? Surely most of them do, so why do I have to repeat it all? Why *should* I repeat it all? People are hearing sad news all through the year, so why add to *their* sadness just because I'm feeling my own?

For weeks, the cards and letters remained a question in my mind, though somehow I could hear John prodding me, urging me to go forward, telling me how important the tradition has been, not just to us but to the many people who've received these hand-done cards over the years.

And so, eventually, I did send out the Christmas cards, all 250 of them. Instead of a separate letter, however, I printed a message within the card, saying that John had died and I would continue the tradition he so loved.

One tradition *not* in question was baking baklava. This I have done for many years. I do much of the baking alone, taking great pleasure in tasting the walnut-sugar mixture so that it's exactly the correct sweetness, then rolling the combination into the phyllo dough.

John always had the first piece, still warm and dripping with the traditional sugar-lemon syrup poured over it immediately after it came out of the oven. He always gave it a thumbs-up, even though there were a couple of years when I—my own harshest critic—felt it could have been better.

The one day I do not bake the baklava alone is when David joins me in the kitchen. He has become a superb cook and baker, and we enjoy our afternoon together, each of us baking one pound of the delicious pastry. We managed to do that again this year, but I felt the difference in my heart as we moved through my kitchen.

Several days before David arrived, I baked the first two of five pounds of baklava, a process that took about five hours in all. After clarifying the salted butter, I made the sugar-lemon syrup and finally ground the walnuts. I mixed the nuts with plenty of sugar, ready for stuffing into sheets of buttered phyllo, three sheets to create each long roll.

Phyllo is extremely tricky to work with, especially if it's not at room temperature. Once I pack the long roll with nuts tightly enough for it to remain stable, I cut the roll into diagonal, bite-size pieces. Each pound of phyllo creates sixty to seventy pieces, which I offer as gifts to friends. It's a long process, but well worth the effort when I see the delight on people's faces as they take that first bite.

I listened to Christmas carols the entire time I stood in the kitchen, hoping that somehow I would find my spirits lifted, by both my activities and the music. But I found it hard to get beyond the sadness of the season. I was feeling extremely lethargic about the entire holiday. Almost the only thing I really wanted to do was just to *be*. I wanted to sit back and allow myself to truly reflect on the loss of John. I think I had managed to keep myself so busy since his death just six months earlier that I had kept much of my grief at bay, and, judging from my conversations with others who've lost loved ones, many do exactly as I've done. But as I experienced the ten-day holiday break from work, I felt the true impact of life without John.

The other night, after a happy dinner with friends and a brief visit to a crowded party, I dreamed I was riding a bicycle with a young man at my side. He was clearly an admirer, but I didn't recognize him. We rode a long way together. I felt the wonder of fresh air in my lungs, and surprisingly I experienced no fatigue at all. At the end of our ride, I said out loud, "I did well, didn't I?"

Does it help to go to parties? I had thought it might, so, though I left early, I knew how important it was to be there, to keep on living.

This morning I was standing in the bathroom, applying

makeup, when without warning my back went into spasm, something that hasn't happened in years. The pain traveled instantly down both legs. I almost screamed. I got on my knees, crawled to my bed, and turned over on my back. I pulled my knees to my chest to try to ease the spasm. John is not here to help me. I am alone.

My immediate feeling was one of self-pity, but that was not going to help me. I crawled back into the bathroom, raised myself carefully to reach for the medicine cabinet, and took two Tylenol. I then made my way back to the bedroom and got onto the bed, where I spent the rest of the day, lying flat on my back. The body remembers. It's a statement I've never forgotten. I've done so well this Christmas, going to Christmas Eve services at the cathedral, being with friends for Christmas Eve and Christmas Day dinners, participating as fully as possible in laughter, conversation, thoughtful exchanges. Now I confront the reality of the afterward, the time away from the happy faces and joyous songs, the time of being by myself. My body reminds me that all the cooking, baking, singing, and socializing cannot distance me from myself. My back spasm calls me back to the reality of loss, forcing me to remember that grief is complicated and long-lasting, forcing me to give attention to my deepest feelings rather than try to stay detached from them. The body remembers.

❧ Grief

Throughout this period since John died, I've been trying to define for myself exactly what grief is. The Oxford dictionary has many definitions, including "mental anguish or sorrow . . . bereavement or bitter regret or remorse." I realize I am in the process of experiencing all of these things. I would add sadness, loneliness, a sense of isolation, self-imposed or otherwise. And, to be honest, some anger, a resentment at having been abandoned.

And what can I do except live through all these things? Continue to put one foot in front of the other. Carry on. Behave normally. Act as though I'm still whole, when a central part of me, which is what John has been for most of my life, is gone.

My daughter and grandchildren wanted me to join them in Boston for Christmas, so I wouldn't be alone. It was a dear suggestion on their part, but one I declined. What I most wanted to do instead was to wake up on Christmas morning in the bed John and I had shared for so many years, the bed I could now imagine our waking up in together, wishing each other a Merry Christmas, perhaps making love before rising, or just holding each other.

But I grieve for those very memories as well, since long before he moved into assisted living, John had moved into another room so that each of us could sleep peacefully. My sadness is filled with the longing for all those nights when we did sleep together, side by side, in the loving warmth of each other's body. In other words, I am grieving not only for the loss of John but for the loss of the beauty that, before his illness descended, we had together.

I am grieving for our youth, for our love, for our happiness, even for our sadness together. The grief is for the joy we experienced when I gave birth to David and then to Jennifer, the immense joy and pride we had in watching those two beautiful children grow into such extraordinary adults. Even now, when I hear inside me their voices or those of their children, I am saying, "I wish John were here."

Yesterday as I was leaving the apartment to go to a friend's house, I heard John say, "Now is there anything you're supposed to take with you?" And there was. I was taking baklava to my friend, which otherwise I might have forgotten. Is the fact that I hear John's voice part of the immediate grieving process? Or will that question, which he asked so often as we were leaving to go out, always be with me?

And what of the duration of grief? Do some of us "get over" the loss more quickly, depending on the circumstances of the death and the duration of the illness? I know John wanted to die. He was finished with the loss of dignity he was experiencing. And therefore I understood and supported him and wanted his wish granted. But the fact that he wanted to die—and I felt strongly about his *right* to die—doesn't diminish the grief I felt when he *did* die, and continue to feel. Death is the ultimate finality, and there is no turning back.

Some, hearing the circumstances of John's death, will view it as an act of suicide, the deliberate taking of one's own life. But I see it as an act of relinquishment, of giving in to the process of dying. He wanted to die. He was ready to die. He could not physically "take" his own life, but he could, as he did, "relinquish" his life, by denying himself food, water, and medication. Should my grief be any less intense because it was his own choice? Should my sadness be lessened because he made his own decision to leave his body behind?

What intrigues me is that John so often talked of "the journey ahead." Indeed, his own book is titled *Onward Journey*. He saw this earthly life as just one part of our being, our coming into existence and our travels toward the end of mortal life as part of a much longer journey, toward something not necessarily God-filled but nevertheless holy.

As I reread parts of his book, his fables, his poetry, I realize how much of his thinking I did not understand. The older he grew, the more complicated he—and his writings—became, somehow almost secretly focused inward. By the time his book was published, Parkinson's disease had so weakened his vocal cords that those attending the book party Jane and David Dixon gave for him could barely hear him speak. When, however, I hear him speak to me now, it is with the strength of his young voice, the very strong voice that when we first met I regarded with such disdain. Now I yearn daily, almost hourly, to hear it again.

With whom, and how, am I to grieve? With my children, who have lost their father? With friends, who ask, again and again, how I am managing? How do I share the grief that comes in waves, or that wakes me in the night? To whom do I say, at those moments, how I long to see John, to hear his voice, to speak of my sadness? It is to him that I want to speak. Only he, after all our years together, can understand, and yet he is not here to hear me.

My back is hurting. It is part of my grief. If he were in this room, he would talk with me about the physical aspects of my grief. He would remind me of all the winters when, anticipating the memories surrounding my parents' deaths, I would experience terrible colds and take to my bed. He would encourage me to rest, to give in to the sense of loss, to allow my feelings to fill my mind rather than to push them away. And now these thoughts are of him.

At one and the same time I dwell on the caring he showed me in our better moments and the loneliness I felt when he chose to shut me out. The memories come together, the goodness, the love, the caring merging with the silence, the rejection, the sense of hopelessness. And what I realize is that that is exactly what my entire life has been about.

*F*inally, relief. The holidays are at an end. The Christmas tree, the wreath, the cards, the poinsettias have all been put away. The tissue paper, ribbons, pie plates, cake rounds are all back in storage. But far more important than that, I will no longer have to listen to people's condolences. They are all kind and solicitous, but each one reminds me that any joy I feel must be tempered by sadness and loss. It's hard to be authentically anything or anyone as I encounter the sadness in people's faces as they remind me, again and again, how hard "the first Christmas" is. I know. I feel it. I'm really trying to move beyond it.

After all, it really isn't the first Christmas I've been without John. Last year, though I spent a good part of the day with him at Brighton Gardens, it was a day of melancholy, quiet, quiet words, watching him sleep, feeding him a mediocre Christmas dinner. I was already "without" him then.

So as the New Year begins, how shall I "be"? I am moving not only beyond the "first" Christmas without him but into a brand-new year, with many challenges and opportunities lying ahead. I am going to be much more involved in Compassion & Choices. I will continue to speak about, specifically, John's death and, more generally, my belief that each of us deserves the right to choose how we die. After I retire, I will travel to other cities to participate with citizens in that debate. This is an opportunity and, indeed, an obligation I feel I must take on in the wake of John's death.

I will continue to be involved with USAgainstAlzheimer's, hoping that we can take Trish Vradenburg's play, *Surviving Grace,* to even more cities. At the same time, I will do all I can to assist in the Parkinson's disease effort, hoping to bring more attention as well as more research dollars to both diseases. And of course, at least for the immediate future, I'll be going on with the daily radio program that means so much to me.

I assume I'll be able to continue with all these activities because my health is good. I have no abnormalities (that I know of—but who can ever really know?), my energy level remains high, and I'm surrounded by good friends of all ages. As time goes on, I observe some of my older friends declining, while my younger ones grow more interesting to me. In fact, I find myself reaching out to friends and neighbors more than I ever allowed myself to do earlier in life. I'm going to expand my home entertaining as much as my strength and my pocketbook allow.

Outside it's drizzling and very gray. There are no people here, just Maxie and me. There is no pressure. I make no social engagements. I feel at peace and spend the day quietly, anticipating my return to work tomorrow.

But thinking about the future without John by my side helping to test or debate various prospects, either with the station or elsewhere, makes me anxious.

Over the years, I've relied so much on his advice and sound judgment. I've been so blessed with the incredible opportunities I've had, working with people I've enjoyed (with a few exceptions, of course). Now, as I look ahead a year or two, I'm both sad and excited. I want to continue to contribute in meaningful ways to the conversations that I believe this country must have, but how much will I enjoy my life away from the daily involvement with journalism?

After Carl Kasell, NPR newscaster for so many years, stopped doing his daily broadcasts on *Morning Edition,* a job that demanded his rising at 3:00 a.m. on weekdays, he said to me and others, "Sleeping in is overrated." Through all these years I've complained about early rising being the bane of my working life. Will I feel as Carl did, once he was free to "sleep in"?

∽ Tragic Death

I attended a funeral yesterday, one of the saddest I've ever been to, and so traumatic—that of a young man, thirty-four years old, who had apparently taken his own life. His mother and father sat devastated in the front row, weeping inconsolably, as friends, relatives, and colleagues spoke of their son's brilliance, humor, and compassion. The synagogue was filled to capacity. I hadn't known this young man, but I felt very deeply the desire to give support to his parents, who are friends of mine. The eulogies were poignant, filled with tears but also funny stories. The speakers remembered his childhood pranks, shared meals, long conversations, all-nighters. One young woman sang his favorite song. And after each remembrance, the parents rose and embraced the presenter, still sobbing.

And then, just a day later, on January 7, 2015, came the horrible bloodshed in Paris. First the killing of twelve people, well-known cartoonists and editors at the offices of *Charlie Hebdo*, a magazine known for its satirical portrayals of religious leaders of all faiths. Members of the police force were also murdered. The two killers were brothers, alleged Muslim extremists. A manhunt ensued. Paris was on lockdown and extremely fearful the next day. The tragic finale came two days later, when another terrorist killed hostages at a kosher grocery store on the eve of the Jewish Sabbath, and the two brothers were finally shot and killed by French police as they ran from a warehouse where they'd been hiding.

That the funeral for the young man who had apparently given up on his life was followed the very next day by the siege in France transformed my first week back in the office after a ten-day holiday from a time of feeling rested into a time of sorrow, horror, and disbelief that our world, both near and far, is in such chaos. We think we can manage our lives in neat and orderly ways, taking care of daily responsibilities, moving through each day with such calm assurance, and then, suddenly, we're reminded of just how fragile life really is.

I grieve for my friends who've lost their beloved son. I grieve for them because I know them. But I also grieve for those hostages, and for everyone else caught in such frightening and fatal situations—people who had no inkling of the disaster awaiting them. Is safety something we can no longer take for granted, even as we walk out of our own doors into our own neighborhoods? Will the people of Paris believe they can ever be safe again? Will the peaceful Muslims of Europe fear that they will now become targets of worldwide wrath, even though they played no part in these horrific acts?

Last night, in the wake of the terror in Paris, I went to dinner at the home of Jewish friends, cookbook author Joan Nathan and her husband, Allan Gerson—I was the one non-Jewish person there. I loved hearing those around me singing the prayerful songs, followed by the words of the Torah. At one point, I asked my hosts and fellow guests whether they believed that what had happened in France might change their thinking about the use of deliberately offensive language, if perhaps we as citizens of a more connected world should approach satire and the use of ugly writings and drawings more cautiously.

What followed was a fascinating and spirited discussion, with many differing views. There were absolutists regarding freedom of speech. Others believed our freedoms might have gone too far. Still others argued that magazines like *Charlie Hebdo* should temper publishing extremely offensive material targeting those in the Islamic world. At the end, people thanked me for raising the question, for leading those around the table to seriously consider such matters, and for the opportunity to consider their own views as they heard from others.

Part of me is glad that John wasn't here to have witnessed what happened in his beloved Paris, the city of his birth. He would have been struck by disbelief and heartache. And he and I undoubtedly would have carried on a fierce discussion about First Amendment rights. His belief was firm: there should be no infringement on those rights, no matter the consequences. However, he would at the same time have acknowledged the unpredictability of human behavior—behavior that can so easily lead to such terrible acts of violence.

So often he and I debated the value of the law in various cases, especially those where I felt human values were being ignored and the *letter* of the law was being followed too strictly. In fact, I went so far as to argue that a non-lawyer should be a sitting member of our Supreme Court, to bring into the debate the human impact of the court's decisions. As a broadcaster, I strongly uphold freedom of speech. However, I'm also concerned about how far that freedom will take us, especially when it allows individuals to threaten, frighten, humiliate, or even drive people to suicide by the use of bullying language.

We're in a new world of super-rapid communication, where

texting and instant messaging can have disastrous results. The *Charlie Hebdo* incident reminds us—once again—that words have power: power to affect us in ways that can enlighten, or power to lead us to carry out acts of destruction. I wish I could be discussing this vital issue with John. Perhaps even he would be modifying his position, given this new world we're all living in.

⤳ Reality

*P*erhaps I'm idealizing him. But over and over again I remember how John always cared for me when I wasn't well: after an operation, experiencing pneumonia, hepatitis from a blood transfusion, even just watching over me when I was down with a bad cold or flu. He was always there. He was a better caregiver than I was.

I remember walking with him on the streets of a peaceful Paris, staying at a beautiful hotel on the Seine, the *bateau-mouche* we enjoyed the first day we arrived. We held hands during the entire cruise, feeling as lucky as two people could ever be. Lovely memories. I try to hold on to them, even as I watch the world around me change from peaceful and safe to threatening and dangerous.

For the most part, the past is a comfortable place for me to dwell. It's so easy to recall the lovely moments, when we were happy together. I choose not to live in the negative past. And I remind myself that there's a certain relief to living on my own, making my own decisions, caring for myself. I relish my independence. I take satisfaction in the way I handle my finances, paying bills on time, watching what I spend, making sure I'm prepared to deal with my taxes. That's all part of a new world for me, and I'm pleased I can carry on.

Yet I still struggle with my feelings of loss, loneliness, and neediness. What I'm realizing more and more, especially each time I come down with yet another bout of cold or flu or sinus infection, is just how dependent I was on John, and how needy a person I am. Several counselors with whom I've dealt over many years have helped me to realize how the lack of understanding and sense of love from my mother may have been part of what led to my seeking out someone who would and could care for me, and provide a permanent and reliable shelter. And certainly, in the beginning, that's precisely what John did for me, going back to that very first date!

Even in the earliest years of our marriage, with his professional workload at its maximum, John did his best to provide that sense of caring and compassion. But later on, my constant need for a demonstration of love and reassurance may have become more than he could handle.

It's a funny thing about marriage. We seek out those who we believe can fulfill us, who can provide us what has been lacking in our childhood. I believe I chose John, and knew instinctively he was the right man for me, because he was so kind and attentive. In the same way, he chose me because he could be my teacher, and I his pupil, adoring him and needing his assistance and guidance all the way. Ultimately, however, when my career took off, and his was on the decline, the very basis for our marriage began to shift, and we struggled to keep our relationship alive.

I remain so grateful that we did stay together, that we were able to support each other, perhaps in ways we might never have imagined at the beginning of our relationship, right to the very end.

⌒ Waves of Grief

T omorrow I leave for Portland, Oregon, for another voice
treatment. From there I'll travel to Boston to see Jennie
and her family. Before John became ill, he enjoyed going with
me to Boston, relishing the time, however brief, spent with the
family. But gradually, as he weakened, he confessed that it was
too much for him. The hassle of going through airport security,
of sleeping in a bed not his own, of being *with* people longer than
he was used to being, discouraged him from making these trips.
There had also been a series of NPR/WAMU cruises, which we
took many times and which he enjoyed immensely. Then on the
last one we took together—to Egypt and Jordan—it was clear
how increasingly difficult it had been for him. At one point, he
was separated from the rest of the group, not realizing he'd wan-
dered away. I worried about him the entire time. In fact, he got
very ill on that last trip, coming down, as many other passengers
did, with the norovirus, which forced him to stay in bed for a
good part of the cruise. After that, he regretfully declined to join
me on these expeditions, saying it had just become too hard for
him. I missed him badly, but at least I was free from the anxiety
of having to watch him so closely.

As I packed for my trip, I was hit with a wave of grief. On
many occasions in the past when I left home, especially without
John, sadness settled into my bones. Whether it was just going
out of town for two days for work or going on the first cruise

without him, I found it was incredibly stressful. Separation anxiety always seemed to undo me.

Today, that feeling is overwhelming. The long trip ahead brings on a deep sense of loneliness, realizing that I now fly alone. When I leave the apartment to run an errand, I leave the radio on, so that I can hear a human voice when I return. I was planning to attend an embassy function this evening, but even after I put on my dress, I thought, I can't do this. I don't have the energy needed to greet people with a smile. I am overcome with grief. Will it always come in waves this way? Will it overcome me totally and unexpectedly? I have no energy. I have no reserves on which to call. But at the same time I know I have to keep going. I feel divided from myself. I wonder whether others who've lost a partner or spouse or child experience these periodic waves they don't see coming.

After my voice treatment in Portland, I rose at 3:00 a.m. to catch an early flight to Boston. What a shot of exuberance that turned out to be! First, in addition to Jennie's wonderful family, there are three dogs, two of them rescues, brought home after weekly volunteer shifts at a local animal shelter. The three all bark simultaneously, galloping from room to room, jumping up not only on people but on furniture. They're all so sweet and adorable!

Since the weather was unbearably cold, we opted for a fire and a thousand-piece jigsaw puzzle, made up of wickedly confusing and interlocking pieces creating a huge mélange of candy bars—every single candy bar I've ever eaten plus some I've never heard of. What fun, and what a challenge! In a total of ten hours, the puzzle was complete and we were hilarious in triumph.

The next day was the big football game determining whether the Patriots would go to the Super Bowl, so Jennie and I made a big pot of chili—without beans. I could scarcely imagine such a thing, but the Rehm-Zide family does not consume legumes—of any kind. Then it was off to the airport, another parting, another separation, but in fact filled with happy memories to carry me homeward.

∼ What Lies Ahead

It was undoubtedly the stopover in Boston that did it, but I got home feeling rejuvenated rather than exhausted, as I ordinarily am after a voice treatment. Being with Benjamin and Sarah and their parents—watching them as they maneuvered through their overlapping schedules—is so uplifting. Young, bright kids with so much life ahead, and such loving parents to guide them.

When I see Jennie and Russell's involvement with their children, I feel regret that John and I were not there in that way for her and David. Times were different. The world was somewhat less child-centric than it is today, and seeing how much fun my daughter and her family have together makes me sad that those years when she was growing up were not happier ones, for all of us. John was so involved in his career while I was struggling to establish my own that we didn't enjoy those years together as I see this family doing.

And now I begin to wind down my career. It's time, I believe, to have a younger voice in the ten-to-noon national spot. I'm not thinking of it as an act of generosity—rather, one of realism. All of media is seeking younger people as listeners, viewers, participants. And by the close of 2016, I'll be eighty years old.

The network and my listeners have grown used to my gravelly, breaking voice, but as I hear the speed with which younger voices permeate broadcast and cable, my sense of my own voice and the difficulties it imposes, both for me and for the listener, begins to take hold. Something new and fresh is needed. It's time for me to move on.

As we at WAMU proceed with discussions about my retirement from the microphone, I realize I'm feeling a growing sense of depression, in regard both to the pending loss of a huge part of my identity and to concerns about my financial future. However, my financial advisers have helped to create a balanced plan for me that should allow me to live in comfort—certainly not luxury—for the rest of my life.

But after what seems a lifetime of delving into issues that are not only interesting but absorbing, I wonder whether I'll be able to find fulfillment in other activities. Every weekday morning I'm forced to slough off some of the emotional heaviness I'm beginning to experience as the red light signaling "on air" goes on. I have to maintain my energy, my interest, my concentration, and for the most part I'm able to do that. Yet as I sit at my desk in my office, a room flooded with light, surrounded by photographs of my husband and family, and hearing our producers as they discuss the program about to begin and the one coming up tomorrow, I know I'm already feeling a sense of profound loss. In the year and a half remaining to me in this position, I must find a way to allow myself both to understand and to accept those feelings while trying to bury them as I go on doing my daily work. So even as I continue to experience the loss of John, I am working to adjust myself in anticipation of the loss of what has been my daily occupation.

There's a conflict raging inside. I cannot imagine very many people, especially those of my age who are healthy and able-bodied, wanting to give up something so precious as work that is so interesting and so fulfilling. Yet I recognize and acknowledge that I am getting tired: tired of having to be "on" all the time; tired of having to awaken so early in the morning; tired of having to go to bed so early at night; tired of having to concentrate so hard each and every day. I know that it's time to retire because I'm slowing down. It's hard to admit that to myself, but I do feel it—I'm more tired at the end of each day than I ever used to be, and I recognize that's natural. But it's hard to give in to this reality, hard to say to myself: Diane, it's time.

Of course, that prospect brings on even more grief. How will I fill the void left after what will be more than thirty-seven years at the radio station that has been at the center of my life? Who will I be? I remain a mother and grandmother, but only at a distance. I remain a woman of strength, of ideas, of energy, so how will I focus the years I have remaining to me?

Today's Easter service at the National Cathedral was the first I've attended without John. As always, the flowers, the music, the sense of celebration was everywhere, and most especially in the sermon given by Bishop Mariann Budde. She is bishop of the Episcopal Diocese of Washington, which includes not only this city but large swaths of Maryland.

Easter, of course, celebrates the resurrection of Jesus of Nazareth, crucified on the cross, according to the New Testament, after he was condemned to death on what we Christians call Good Friday. On the third day, the tomb where he'd been laid was found by Mary Magdalene to be empty, with only the shroud in which he'd been wrapped when taken from the cross still remaining.

Bishop Mariann (as she prefers to be called) spoke of how

all of us have experienced some loss, some regret, some major sadness in our lives, and how that feeling of loss may dwell with us for long periods, even a lifetime. But, she said, all of us have it within ourselves to move on, to experience a resurrection, to know life in a different way from what it was before our loss; life without that person or that body of work or that major element that had previously been a central part of our existence.

I thought of John, and how much he loved this service of Easter, singing so joyfully the hymns celebrating what became the foundation of Christianity, the resurrection of Christ Jesus. I thought of John's ability to listen, to be exquisitely conscious of what others around him were saying and even feeling. I thought of his extraordinary kindness to others—the beggars on the street whom I would pass while John unfailingly stopped to offer a dollar or two. I thought of his own conversion experience there in New York, after a lifetime of rejecting Christ, at the Church of St. Thomas the Doubter.

And then I began to wonder about my own transitions, not only from married woman to widow but also from national radio talk-show host to . . . who knows what?

Bishop Mariann talked about herself in terms of questioning what comes next, looking ahead, thinking of a new path as a step forward, recognizing and accepting the loss of what was but allowing new ideas to take hold, feeling the courage to face the unknown, and knowing that we can do what it takes to be ready, to be, as she put it, "poised for resurrection."

Her sermon spoke directly to me, addressing the challenges and opportunities and feelings lying ahead of me. Relief at freedom. Ability to move forward and adjust. A year and a half away.

It should be an occasion for sadness but also for excitement. Feeling at times like a frightened child. The little girl in me comes out and says, "I'm scared!"

Then real life intervenes. A leak developed in the penthouse above my condo, and water leaked into my living room ceiling. Now there's a four-by-six-foot opening exposing pipes, pulling out insulation, my living room walls devoid of art, the girandoles down from the wall, the piano and all furniture moved out of the way. A nightmare. Good thing I wasn't planning an Easter brunch!

⤳ Planning for the Future

I don't believe I have the courage John showed at the end of his life. It was extraordinarily brave of him to make the decision he made, and to carry it out. I'm not sure I would have the willpower to deprive myself of food and water for a period of ten days. Rather, if I find myself facing a prolonged and painful illness, I will seek an organization or an individual to help me carry out my wishes. As I've said before, the fact that we in this country, with the exception of a few states, continue to deny individuals the right to choose to be helped in dying seems to me a violation of the most basic human right.

I was extremely heartened by the unanimous decision, in February 2015, of the Supreme Court of Canada to strike down laws banning physician-assisted suicide for patients with "grievous and irremediable" medical conditions. The Court wrote: "The prohibition on physician-assisted dying infringes the right to life, liberty and security of the person in a manner that is not in accordance with the principles of fundamental justice." The Canadian Medical Association established a new policy that allows physicians to "follow their conscience when deciding whether to provide medical aid in dying."

Even more recently, a case in Victoria, British Columbia, is grappling with the issue of whether a nursing home can deny the family of a woman who has Alzheimer's the right to stop providing nourishment and liquids. The patient, in her pre-Alzheimer's illness, signed documents stating her wish *not* to have her life prolonged with food or liquid should she become incapable of caring for herself. But the institution in which this woman resides believes its own standards and beliefs supersede those of the patient and her family.

That is what I fear: that my desire to take control of my life and end my own suffering will not be honored.

Since John's death, I've done several radio programs about aid in dying or, as its critics prefer to call it, assisted suicide. I've heard many people express very strong views both for and against a terminally ill person's right to take his or her own life using prescribed medications. So I'm aware that there are many people who believe a patient's desire to die can be alleviated by simply providing appropriate care. As California debated its own End of Life Option Act, opponents like Ira Byock, MD, a palliative-care physician, agreed that "Americans have a Constitutional right to refuse life-prolonging treatments." He went on to express his concerns, however, about a physician's involvement in ending a patient's life by saying that "there's a big difference between being allowed to die of your disease and having a doctor intentionally end your life." He argued for more education of young physicians in palliative care and managing pain.

Atul Gawande, in his book *Being Mortal: Medicine and What Matters in the End,* acknowledges that medical school textbooks teach very little about aging, frailty, or dying. He writes, "The purpose of medical schooling was to teach how to save lives, not how to tend to their demise." He argues, as does Dr. Byock, that medical studies must be improved to incorporate more focus on palliative care to relieve prolonged suffering. However, during a recent hour on my program, when I asked for his thoughts on a physician's assisting patients to die, he said, "I'm not there yet."

I would wish to be provided with medication with which to end my life at the time of my choosing. There may be considerable pain that factors into my decision, or it may be that I fear loss of my ability to lead what to my mind is a meaningful life. If I'm unable to feed myself, to toilet myself, to stand or walk on my own, to make rational choices, I want my family to under stand that it's time for me to go—that it's my decision for myself and no one else's.

I respect the arguments made by Dr. Byock and those who believe that life should end naturally. However, I've known of too many instances where "naturally" meant after years of suffering, not only for the individual but for the family. And I do believe the family must be taken into account. I wouldn't wish to put my family through the extended ordeal of my dying. When the time comes to end my life, I will give thanks for all I have had, for all I have been given, and hope to go peacefully, with the help of a physician.

On November 5, 2014, barely five months after John died, Patricia Harrison, president and CEO of the Corporation for Public Broadcasting, invited me to attend a dinner to discuss Parkinson's disease. There were twenty of us seated in a private room of a Georgetown restaurant, Cafe Milano. All of us were asked to speak briefly about our own involvement with Parkinson's. When it came to me, I stood and spoke about the fact that John had reached the end of his battle with the disease by starving himself, refusing water and all medications. I spoke briefly about how difficult it was to watch him withdraw from life, albeit on his own terms, and stated my own wish that he had had an easier and more compassionate end-of-life experience. I went on to say that I hoped eventually we would all have a right to choose when and how we die, with the aid of a physician, if we have been deemed terminally ill.

As fate would have it, present at that dinner was Michael Rosenwald, a reporter for the *Washington Post*. He approached me after dinner and asked whether he might call me to talk further about John's death and our experience as he chose to die. I agreed to speak with him and told him then just how strongly I felt about the issues surrounding aid in dying.

Several weeks later, Mike came to my office, where we sat and talked for nearly ninety minutes, going back over the very first conversations John and I had had regarding our belief in the right to die and our promise to help each other when the time came.

On Sunday, February 15, 2015, the *Post* published his front-page article titled "Rehm's Topic: Death with Self-Determination." Mike wrote of my frustration at the inability of those dying in most states to achieve a peaceful end. The article mentioned that I would be the featured guest at three dinners planned by Compassion & Choices (C & C) to share my experiences and to hear from others about their own end-of-life wishes. Guests were asked to pay $2,500 per person, with all proceeds going to C & C.

After people at WAMU and top executives of the distributor of my program, NPR, read the article, as did the NPR ombudsman, who said she believed that attending such dinners violated NPR's ethical standards, they asked to meet with me. The NPR executives and their specialists came to our studios to talk with me and our station's general manager, J. J. Yore. They expressed concerns about my attending these paid dinners, suggesting that my presence would raise doubts about my journalistic integrity, about my ability to hold discussions on the subject of aid in dying as an unbiased host.

Together, we finally agreed that I would attend the remaining two already fully subscribed dinners, but no more. I told them I was saddened by their belief that I should cut short my active participation in these dinners but would reluctantly accede to their wishes.

Mike Rosenwald wrote a follow-up piece for the *Washington Post*. It was headlined FOLLOWING CRITICISM, NPR HOST DIANE REHM SCALES BACK EFFORTS IN RIGHT-TO-DIE DEBATE. He noted that NPR and WAMU had issued a joint statement saying I would continue to host shows on the topic but would remind my audience of my affiliation with Compassion & Choices.

Then, a month later, on March 15, 2015, came a lead editorial in the Sunday edition of the *New York Times*, the first sentence of which read: "Last year, the radio host Diane Rehm watched in agony as her husband, John, starved to death over the course of 10 days." The editorial went on to discuss current laws allowing health-care providers in five states—Oregon, Washington, Vermont, New Mexico, and Montana—to assist in hastening the death of terminally ill patients, and urged other lawmakers around the country to consider how successfully and responsibly Oregon's Death with Dignity Act has been carried out since it went into effect in 1997. The law "gives doctors the right to prescribe a lethal dose of medication to patients who are terminally ill and who have been advised of their alternatives, such as hospice care. The law provides layers of safeguards to ensure proper diagnosis of the disease, determine a patient's competency to make the decision, and protect against coercion."

And so, without fully realizing what was happening, with those articles and that editorial, I had emerged as what the *Washington Post* called a "key force in the right to die debate."

The fact that laws had now changed in six states indicated the beginning of a change in thinking about this profoundly serious subject. Lawmakers in twenty-six other states and the District of Columbia had in recent months introduced so-called aid-in-dying bills to make such a humane option available to millions of Americans at a time when the nation's population of older adults is growing. This past June the California state senate voted to allow physician-assisted dying after the California Medical Association withdrew its objections, and Governor Jerry Brown signed the bill into law. I pray that this will signal the way for other states to follow suit. And with Canada's Supreme Court decision, I am optimistic the issue will gain further traction among states in this country.

Each and every one of us should have the right to choose. The idea of suffering as being noble does not persuade me that extending life for the sake of someone else's religious beliefs or social philosophy is fair or even reasonable. Let each of us make our own decision.

Unlike the Netherlands, where euthanasia is permitted when an individual is terminally ill and a doctor is present to carry out the act, these six states allow doctors to prescribe medications only to patients who have been deemed to be within six months of death. At least two doctors must make that declaration. The individual might or might not choose to *take* the medication, but—as has been said many times by Barbara Coombs Lee, president of Compassion & Choices, which lobbied for the groundbreaking law in Oregon—having that medication in hand provides a sense of comfort and control over one's own life.

In November 2014, when Brittany Maynard decided she would take her own life after being diagnosed with inoperable and terminal brain cancer, she moved from California to Oregon with her husband and family to put herself in the care of doctors there.

Brittany declared she would end her life on November 1, 2014, with her husband and mother by her side. And she did exactly that, reportedly waking that morning with her decision firm. She indicated that the time had come to take the life-ending medication. In her public statements before her death, she advocated for aid in dying for all who make such a choice. She chose to end her own life without suffering the final degradations, the ultimate decline, in a bed of her own, with her family supporting her and standing by her side. This was my husband's choice, and I felt precisely the same way he did. But he was denied this option.

I do believe I can be of use in this very controversial movement, carrying on for both myself and John. It feels ironic that I have been thrust into an ambiguous situation with regard to my employment. Somehow the right to die seems such a basic issue, one that perhaps should not be left up to state legislators. Why should someone who may have a totally different set of beliefs and values from my own have the legal authority to decide whether I should continue to live and suffer or to die peacefully? It makes very little sense to me. And the idea of a so-called slippery slope is disproven by the fact that, since the Oregon Death with Dignity law was first passed in 1998, a total of only 1,327 patients have received life-ending prescriptions, of whom 859 have actually taken their own lives.

As for life-prolonging measures, I have decided that if, on physical examination by my physician or via self-examination, I discover a lump in my breast, it's too late in my life for me to undergo the traumatic and painful procedures associated with either surgery or radiation and chemotherapy, or both, although pain isn't, and has never been, for me a deciding factor in treatment. These treatments might very well succeed in prolonging my life, for which I would certainly be grateful, but not at the cost of the rigorous and debilitating effects that such treatments would likely entail. I've been fortunate to have lived a healthy life, with only minor bumps along the way, and I'm content with what I've had and am ready to go before life becomes a misery.

Needless to say, this is a highly personal choice, and one determined by my age and circumstances. Certainly if I were younger, even by ten or fifteen years, or had a family dependent on me, or if John were still with me, I might have a very different perspective. I completely understand and sympathize with those who are determined to hang on to life as long as is remotely possible—Susan Sontag is a formidable example. But paradoxically I prefer to go when I still have something to live for—and on my own terms.

I have begun to formulate an idea. Just as John's death was an ending to that chapter of my life, by his death he has actually given me a final gift, the impetus to carry on in a new and vital way. Once freed from my station's and NPR's ethical constraints, I shall do all I can to promote the right of aid in dying. When invited, I will speak out on what I believe should be our right to choose, and help to formulate ways to communicate that idea to members of state legislatures and to the general public. I believe this country is at a tipping point with regard to this issue, much as it was with gay marriage several years ago. And now that a chance meeting with a *Washington Post* reporter has given my position on the issue a voice, I shall use it.

I find it interesting that, even as I consider what lies ahead, I begin thinking about my own death—not in a morbid way, but wondering whether it will come sooner rather than later. How long do I have to live? And how long do I really *want* to live? How soon might I succumb to some disease or disorder lurking or developing within me? Do other widows and widowers wonder whether they really *want* to go on after a life partner dies?

For some time I focused on what I believed would be the death of my career. But no longer. Now I know I do not have to give in to self-pitying thoughts, because I do plan to go on. I plan to have new experiences, meet new people, travel to new places. Most of all, I plan to continue to be a fully engaged human being.

⮏ Closure

This week I received a card from the widow of Malcolm Browne, a Pulitzer Prize–winning *New York Times* journalist and photographer and a dear friend of John's when they attended Friends Seminary together in New York City. Malcolm also died after a long battle with Parkinson's disease. The last time he and John spoke on the phone was at least a year before Malcolm's death. At the time, John reported that Malcolm was suffering greatly, wheelchair bound, and barely able to speak.

Something his widow, Le Lieu, wrote to me when John died really struck me. She said, "Malcolm died two years ago and I miss him even more." I, too, am finding that, as the days go by, I miss John "even more." I think I had anticipated that the grief would be extremely intense immediately after he died, and that, as the days went by, that grief would grow less and less intense, especially because he'd been gone from my daily existence for so long before he died. Instead, what I find is that I spend more and more time *thinking* about him, seeing and hearing flashbacks of our time together. I rarely think of the sad times, but memories of our good times keep running through my brain, demanding attention, making me smile. Then, even as I smile, the sadness overcomes me, as I wish there were a way to redo so much of our lives together.

Malcolm's wife, two years after his death, misses him even more. I think that's what's happening to me as well. Had John died a more peaceful and comfortable death, I wonder whether

I'd feel different. I also wonder whether some of us believe there's a "right way" for us to grieve; whether, given that so many of us have read Elisabeth Kübler-Ross's book about the stages of grief, we've come to believe there are certain designated periods allotted first to denial, followed by anger, bargaining, depression, and finally acceptance. But even in these very early months following John's death, I seem to follow no pattern whatsoever. Some days I feel just fine, I smile, I laugh, I interact happily with my friends and neighbors. Other days I'm sad. Still others, I'm *really* down and can't talk to a soul. I just want to be alone with my memories.

Is there something wrong with this? Somehow, I don't think so. I think it's my own way of dealing with a profound loss, the most profound since my parents died, sixty years ago. How can I not be on this roller coaster of grief when each day feels different, when some thought or image or sound reminds me of John and the life we lived together?

No one, thank goodness, has said to me, "It's time to move on." And I sincerely hope no one ever does, because I know that some part of me will grieve forever. That doesn't mean I'll be weeping or wailing on a daily basis. What it does mean is that there will always be a deep sadness in my heart for the loss of John, for the life we built together, for the glorious moments of love we shared, and even for some of the most profoundly difficult moments we experienced together.

I don't believe in closure. What does it really mean? Does it mean the closing of a door, the locking up of memories, the refusal to allow a flow of consciousness that may involve some measure of grief? There's rarely been a day since my mother and father died when I haven't thought of them. How could I possibly experience something like "closure" about my husband's death? Can there be such a thing as closure in regard to the death of a child?

Recently there have been several airline crashes into the sea, one in which no trace of plane or bodies has been recovered, another in which a black box has finally been found, along with the remains of the plane and dozens of bodies. And a third where it was determined a pilot deliberately crashed a plane carrying 148 passengers into a mountain. Will those who've lost loved ones in such disasters ever achieve "closure," even if the bodies of their beloved relatives or friends are recovered? I doubt it.

Death is final, but grief is ongoing. The extent to which we experience it may or may not depend on the depth of love or even the depth of regret we feel. But it is our own experience. No one else can define it for us. In fact, perhaps grieving, at some level, is the ongoing effort to continue to live with those we've lost. When the tears flow from my eyes, I can almost hear John speaking to me, comforting me, and feel him drawing me close. It's my grief, my very own, and I know that as I experience it and allow it to be part of who and what I am, I shall grow.

⤳ Who Am I?

For fifty-four years I have been a wife. Now I am a widow. Am I someone new? I was part of a couple. Now I am a single person. When we married, if I had a question, John could answer it. Now if I forget something, who will remind me, or who will know what I mean to say? What if, at some point, I develop dementia? Who will remember for me? Who will remember what I have forgotten? Where will my memories be? Will they reside at least in part in my children, whose lives are busy creating their own memories? And what of my grandchildren? They will know who I am through only the barest of their parents' memories.

For the first time I am struck by the realization that who I am is in large part a lifetime of memories, from early childhood on. Where do those memories go when we die?

I once asked John if he could have any time of his life back again, which years would they be? What were the favorite years of his life? It didn't take him very long to answer that they were his teenage years at Friends Seminary. I was not surprised. He had lived alone with his mother during those years at Friends, an only child whose mother doted on him.

Through all these years I've defined myself as wife, mother, friend, and radio broadcaster. As I move into this new phase, who and what shall I be? If no longer wife, surely still mother, but in very different ways from those of earlier years. I've learned from my children to keep my distance, to listen to each of them more carefully, and to honor their decisions without probing.

As a grandmother, I can have more fun. Should the children come and stay with me for a short or long period of time, I can learn from them and they, one hopes, from me. We can enjoy each other in ways I didn't allow myself to enjoy my children when they were young, because I was so tied up in knots about my career and my relationship with John.

When John and I first walked into this apartment, gauging whether it might be right for us, the first words he whispered to me were "Diane, look at the light!" And indeed, the apartment was totally free from shadow, wide windows opening onto parkland fourteen stories below, sunshine pouring into every room.

I found myself thinking about those first moments in the apartment when, last night, I began wondering whether John had "seen the light" as he lay dying. And, alternatively, whether he is telling me, from wherever he is, to "look at the light." To look ahead, to plan, to investigate with excitement what possibilities lie ahead. He planned carefully for his family, so that each of us could move forward at different stages of our lives.

Now, in this new place in which I find myself, I hope I, too, can see the light ahead, that I am open to new avenues, new views of life, knowing that what is past lies only in my heart, and that possibilities of the future, if I allow them to enter, await me.

Last night, after I'd written about the light he saw and the light ahead, I dreamed I saw John as a young man, standing totally naked in a bathroom while I lay in bed looking through the door watching him shave. Then he came to me and took my arm, which was inside a red knit sweater. He began unraveling the edge of the sleeve, stitch by stitch and row by row, until he had removed about an inch of the sleeve. In the dream, I asked him why he was doing that, why he was in effect changing the look and length of my sleeve. His response: "Because it looks more modern this way."

However one is given to interpret dreams, the message I took from this one was that he was encouraging me in my decision to move on from the daily work of broadcasting, to search for something new, something "more modern." Sometimes I dream and don't remember. This dream was powerful and totally recalled. Thinking about it gives me a measure of comfort and reassurance. John is with me, if only in my dreams, easing me into new pathways, taking my hand along the way, helping me to learn to be unafraid.

Years ago, when I first began my broadcast career, I was so deathly afraid every morning before going on the air that I was almost paralyzed inside. No one other than John knew that; no one seemed to notice it. He and I talked about this fear a great deal, and one day he said to me, "Just let the fear in. Don't try to fight it. Let it be a part of who you are." Words I shall never forget.

So now I move forward, still grieving, but knowing that my husband will always be part of my life, a huge part, and I shall love him forever.

⟿ A Mass Memorial Service

O n April 26, 2015, nearly a year after John's death, I attended a service for family members and friends of those who'd donated their bodies to George Washington University's medical school. The service was produced by the first-year medical students, the class of 2018, to express their gratitude to the donors and loved ones. In the program, they wrote:

> It is often said that our donors were our first patients, and we believe this to be true. Your loved one has given us an education both inside and outside of the classroom whose value cannot be overstated, and this is an act of graciousness we will honor throughout our careers.

John would have loved the service, one of music, dance, and poetry. He would have loved the reading of the names, first name and last initial only, to preserve anonymity. He would have remembered that Jennie had called the gentleman on whose body she was privileged to work Herc, short for Hercules, because he was such a large and presumably strong man. He would have appreciated hearing of the joy of discovery about which these young students spoke, their wonder at the variety of our species, the intimacy of the relationship between student and subject, the reality of recognizing the body as a miraculous work of art. One student spoke of being humbled and inspired by the realization that "the pain passes, but the beauty remains." Another said she had gained reverence not only for life but for death, and this service would help her as she moves forward to contemplating her own mortality.

I, too, was inspired by these students, their reflections, and the honor with which they viewed the human beings whose lives they could not know but whose bodies they were touching, holding, examining with such care and gentleness. John R. would have been pleased to have made his donation.

M y career has given me extraordinary gratification, more than I could ever have imagined it would. Being on the radio for more than thirty-five years, doing a program I first inherited and then made my own, creating something new and exciting, has given me immense satisfaction. I have not only met and talked with the most fascinating people in the world but learned from all of them.

Early on in my broadcasting days I realized that the way I learn is in a one-on-one environment, when I feel comfortable and in control not only of myself but of my surroundings. I love guiding the conversation. I'm good at listening, and I listen very carefully—that's part of the learning process for me. I didn't go to college, but I've used my time in the studio to learn about the world. Science, literature, politics, medicine, the environment—I've gleaned it all in my own learning laboratory, sitting before a microphone with the ability and courage to ask whatever I wanted to ask, and to probe more deeply whenever my questions were not responded to clearly and forthrightly. I'll miss that daily learning opportunity! But I will replace it.

Certainly there are classes I could attend, but I know of myself that I'm bored by lectures. I can't stand one-way communication. One of the things that have made me love my work so much is that it's always been a real conversation.

Some of us approach the thought of retirement with joy and relief. I know John did. Having worked as an attorney for forty years, he had grown weary of the minute-by-minute record keeping and the focus on the monetary elements of each encounter. He wanted to be free from the daily obligations connected to clients and their issues. He wanted to be in charge of his own daily existence.

Susan Stamberg said how much happier and more relaxed her husband was after he retired from his government work, and how his relationship with both her and their son improved after retirement. Roger Mudd has reminded me that, once retirement comes, the invitations, the phone calls, the attention from the outside world ceases. One moves to a different kind of existence.

I think of those whose work has been physically strenuous, whose muscles have ached at the end of every day, or those who've had to endure jobs that sucked the life out of them, just to put bread on the table. Their retirement must feel like a blessing from heaven when it finally comes, delivering them from the hardships and even pain of what work has been for them.

I've been one of the lucky ones. I know I will step away from my daily occupation with reluctance, but my body is still strong, not weakened by years of hard labor. I know that the experiences and relationships I've grown used to will change, and that I will no longer have the recognition I've enjoyed over these many years, the compliments, the displays of deference and special courtesies. I've tried to make light of the specialness, telling myself it's really not important to me. Yet deep down, I know I've grown to enjoy it.

There will be the loss of my daily interaction with the most prominent and knowledgeable people from around the country and around the world, the excitement of sitting down with them. Most important will be a loss of immediate connectedness to the world. My professional life has been perfect for me, as though the gods knew I was a sponge, ready to soak up everything everyone had to tell me, and then gave me the freedom to pick and choose among all the opinions and suggestions I'd heard. It's been a career I would never have dreamed for myself, and yet I've had it all this time.

When I began working at age sixteen as a file clerk at the old Hecht Company here in Washington, I knew that I wanted to earn not only a salary but also praise—for being the fastest, most accurate file clerk my boss had ever seen. And I was. I wanted to stand out. I was there every Wednesday afternoon after school, and all day each Saturday. My supervisor was always delighted to see me, especially if there were filing tasks that no one else had been able to accomplish. There were days when she would ask me to come in for extra hours, which I was proud of and happy to do because it was the only way I could earn spending money—for clothes, for basketball games, to go out with my friends.

When I went to work as a secretary after graduation from high school, I know I did my job well. Each of my supervisors told me so. I enjoyed their praise and was rewarded with promotions to better-paying positions. I've always wanted and needed praise, perhaps to make up for what I felt I didn't receive as a child. Then again, very few of us ever receive "enough" praise.

So where will that satisfaction come from, if not from a job well done? The answer is I will learn to feed it to myself, knowing that very little of the recognition I've had will continue to come from the outside world.

Of course I will miss my public platform enormously, but I also know I'll find new ways to enjoy life and new things to achieve.

Determination is one of my strongest characteristics. It has led me to persevere, to convince others to believe in me and what I can accomplish. Even at my age, I know there is another chapter ahead, one that will allow me to work in ways that will not only satisfy me but will also be of help to others. Whether it will be by speaking out on causes in which I believe, such as aid in dying, or appearing in Trish Vradenburg's play about Alzheimer's disease, or helping somehow with the Parkinson's disease effort, I believe I will find ways to do whatever I need to do to feed my soul, to keep me going, to stay involved with the world, to find a new place in it for myself. John would expect that of me, and I expect it of myself. And ultimately, I am certain, it will help me to discover who I am, now that I am on my own.

A nniversaries have always been important to me. I can feel them coming weeks before they occur. Thinking back, I believe these sensitivities began after my mother died on New Year's Day, 1956. My father also died on a holiday, November 11, then called Armistice Day, now Veterans Day. As I've written, from that time on, as those dates approached, I would find my neck tightening, my headaches appearing more frequently, the spasms in my back coming on with greater regularity. Added to those dates were the Christmas holidays, always anxiety-producing, reminding me of the loneliness I had experienced as a child, when I never received whatever it was I had been longing for.

I mark these anniversaries each year, remembering both the sadness and relief I experienced with my parents' deaths, knowing that, for the first time in my life, I was free to make my own decisions without fear of wounding either of them. Somewhere deep inside, I realized I had become an orphan, yet old enough and strong enough to carry on.

In the Syrian Orthodox Church, in which I and my children were baptized, the ritual of a service marking the end of a forty-day mourning period was both useful and, in some ways, distressing, forcing me to go back, to re-experience my parents' deaths, to mourn again with my aunts, uncles, cousins, and friends, all of whom felt deeply the deaths of Eugenie and Wadie Aed, just

eleven months apart. I can remember one of my aunts screaming bitterly as we were leaving the cemetery after my father's
burial next to my mother, "Take him, Eugenie, he's yours now."

One year later, on each anniversary, there is yet another service marking the day of death. Each of these is presumably to
help us face the sense of loss and deprivation that death brings.
And perhaps for all these years I *have* been in denial about the
intense grief I experienced when these deaths actually occurred,
feeling too much relief and not enough of the sadness and even
anger that lay deep within me.

I think too of the sea of black: black dresses, hats, shoes, suits,
ties, armbands, all to remind not only those around us but even
ourselves that we are in mourning, reminders of the reality of
the death experience and of loss. In other cultures, the rituals
may look and sound different, but the purpose is the same: to
mourn. In Japan, for example, mourners wear white clothing
rather than black. Some things change for the better: going to
funerals now in these less Victorian-bound days, I witness a sea
of color and style, I hear joyful music, rites of celebration rather
than of mourning.

Now I am facing, indeed steeling myself against, the realization that the first anniversary marking John's death is here. And
there are no prescribed ways to help me get through that day.
There are no gatherings, no church services, no celebrations of
his life.

I am determined to go to work on June 23, determined to
carry on with my life the way I ordinarily do, not to sit at home
and brood. And I do exactly that, going through the course of

my day in the usual way. But as the week progresses, my spirits go downhill. Perhaps because I was guarding myself so much against the day itself that finally, after it is over, I let down my defenses and spiral into depression, not wanting to speak with anyone, not wanting to *be* with anyone. Two days *after* the anniversary, I want only to be at home, by myself, alone with Maxie. I tell my producers I will not be at work.

My children call and e-mail me, as well as a few friends who remember the date. "How are you?" they ask. And always, my answer is, "I'm okay." No better, no worse, just okay.

Now I am truly a widow, having lived through an entire year without my spouse. It has been a year of holidays spent with friends instead of family, of celebrations, accomplishments, and too many funerals. It has been a year filled with moments when it was difficult to concentrate, when I deliberately tried to dismiss thoughts of sadness, struggling to allow myself to really know or understand what I was thinking and feeling. I went through the entire year distracted, to say the least.

A few days prior to the anniversary, on the day other families celebrated Father's Day, I went down to the storage area in our building to look for some specific documents. Though I never found what I was seeking, I did find file drawer after file drawer filled with history, with so many reminders of fifty-four years of marriage.

I went through many of the documents John studied to qualify as a docent for the Freer and Sackler Galleries, as well as other papers related to his long and impressive legal career, and his extensive poetry manuscripts, many of which appeared in his book, *Onward Journey*. There were materials from his ten years at Wesley Theological Seminary, carefully indexed, neatly arranged in notebooks.

As I went through box after box, I was thrilled to come across photos of John as a young man, smiling, healthy, and vigorous. In that moment, on Father's Day, I was glad to be reminded of all that we had had together, and of the many years we had loved and supported each other.

John is no longer physically here beside me, and his death has left a huge emptiness in my life. But I know I have grown during this past year. I've had to become increasingly self-reliant. Every day I've managed to deal with such minor problems as leaks throughout the living-room ceiling. Not long ago I made a major on-air blunder involving Presidential candidate Bernie Sanders, for which I issued a public apology. And I watched in horror as the brutal massacre of innocent churchgoers in Charleston, South Carolina, unfolded. In the past, any or all of those experiences could have made me crumble. But I didn't. I had to be strong, and I have *been* strong. And I hope that as I move forward, I will find ways to give strength to others.

I listen to the radio a great deal when I'm here in the apartment alone. Listening to a recent TED Talk, I heard several people speak about how time seems to speed up as we grow older. One person spoke in particular about how the older we grow, the more we learn to savor each moment, living *in* each moment, and letting go of the less important details of life. I'm trying.

My wedding ring remains on the third finger of my left hand. I will never take it off. When the time comes, I hope my son or my daughter keeps it, as a symbol of the love and respect John and I had for each other, a symbol of the strength with which I pray they will both carry on and will give to their own children.

Of course, I realize that it's too late in my life to begin again. But I know that in this last year I've become a more positive person, concentrating on so much in life that is good, rather than wasting time concentrating on petty issues or grievances. I can only hope that this is the message I convey to those around me.

ACKNOWLEDGMENTS

I am so grateful to my editor, Bob Gottlieb, for his incredibly detailed attention to this book. He pushed and prodded me to think more deeply and carefully, and then read through the unfolding manuscript many times. I have nothing but love and admiration for his kindness and care.

Also, of course, I am grateful to Sonny Mehta, the head of Alfred A. Knopf, and to the devoted and consummately effective Paul Bogaards, who has been one of my champions for many years.

And at Knopf to Lydia Buechler, Ellen Feldman, Iris Weinstein, Lorraine Hyland, Audrey Silverman, and Jessica Purcell.

To Roger Mudd, Susan Stamberg, and Eleanor Clift, for their unstinting generosity and wisdom.

Anne Stonehill read one of the early versions of the book and helped me through some hard decisions with her gentle but firm approach.

Throughout this long and difficult period, David and Mary Beth Busby have been by my side, loving and supporting both John and me.

Trish and George Vradenburg have understood and helped me deal with the highs and lows, and have fed me with both food and love.

And I shall always cherish the love and support of the producers of *The Diane Rehm Show*, most especially throughout these many years Sandra Pinkard.

And finally, I am thankful for the understanding and support of my children, David and Jennifer, who wanted only a gentle passing for their father and a sense of peace for their mother.